**PREPARE CURRICULUM** *Implementation Guide*

# SOCIAL PERCEPTION TRAINING

*Mark Amendola & Robert Oliver, Series Editors*

KNUT KORNELIUS GUNDERSEN ▪ BØRGE STRØMGREN ▪ LUKE MOYNAHAN

# RESEARCH PRESS
PUBLISHERS

2612 North Mattis Avenue, Champaign, Illinois 61822
800.519.2707 / researchpress.com

**RESEARCH PRESS**
PUBLISHERS

Copyright © 2013 by Mark Amendola and Robert Oliver

7   6   5   4   3       14   15   16   17   18

PDF versions of forms and handouts  included in this book are available for download on the book webpage at **www.researchpress.com/downloads**

*Prepare* and *Skillstreaming* are the registered copyright of Research Press. *Aggression Replacement Training* and *ART* are the registered copyrights of Dr. Barry Glick.

"Cognitive Distortions," on page 75, is adapted by permission from *Teaching Adolescents to Think and Act Responsibly: The EQUIP Approach,* © 2012 by A. M. DiBiase, J. C. Gibbs, G. B. Potter, & M. R. Blount, Champaign, IL: Research Press (www.researchpress.com).

"Right Time and Place" illustrations, on page 80, are reprinted by permission from *I Can Problem Solve: An Interpersonal Cognitive-Behavioral Problem-Solving Program– Intermediate Elementary Grades,* © 2001 by M. B. Shure, Champaign, IL: Research Press (www.researchpress.com).

Copies of this book may be ordered from Research Press at the address given on the title page.

Composition by Jeff Helgesen
Cover design by McKenzie Wagner, Inc.
Printed by Edwards Brothers Malloy

ISBN 978-0-87822-680-1
Library of Congress Control Number 2013946195

# Contents

# Figures and Tables

**Figures**

**Tables**

# Foreword

> *The optimal intervention package is never final or complete . . . intervention approaches must perpetually evolve.* —Arnold P. Goldstein

The legacy of Arnold P. Goldstein (1933–2002) spans a remarkable career, blending science with practice to address the most pressing problems of modern youth. The bookends of Arnie's shelf of writings both concern the theme of lasting behavior change. A half century ago, he joined Kenneth Heller and Lee Sechrest as they mined experimental and cognitive research for secrets of how learning endures. In two final books, he set the challenge for the decades ahead: What methods yield lasting change? And how do we engage resistant youth as partners in the process of change?

There are 300 approaches to control student violence, Arnie mused, most based on hearsay, hope, and desperation. While such behavior is challenging to change, most real-world programs are punitive, permissive, or defeatist. For example, he questioned attempts in recent years to portray gangs as narrowly pathological, thereby justifying coercive policies. All adolescents seek out peers for satisfaction, and gang membership is seldom exclusively destructive, but offers camaraderie, pride, excitement, and identity.

The strengths perspective was central to Arnie's philosophy. Seeing potential in all youth motivated his efforts to turn negative peer groups into "prosocial gangs." He was intrigued by the idea that youth themselves may be credible experts on delinquency. This respect for the voices of youth was exemplified in his book *Delinquents on Delinquency* (Goldstein, 1990). Always open to multiple perspectives, he saw ordinary knowledge as a useful adjunct to professional scientific knowledge.

While some feared that aggregating troubled youth for treatment would lead to peer deviance training, Arnie welcomed the opportunity to work with delinquents as a group. It was his understanding of the power of the friendship group that enabled Aggression Replacement Training (ART) to penetrate the gang culture (Goldstein & Glick, 1987). He recognized the potential of building positive youth cultures through peer helping. In fact, he cited research showing that youth were more motivated to participate in skill instruction if they thought they could use this information to help their peers, a concept that served as the foundation of the EQUIP Program (Gibbs, Potter, & Goldstein, 1995).

From Arnie's earliest writings, respectful relationships were recognized as the foundation of all successful helping encounters. This universal principle made his interventions relevant across diverse domains of education, prevention, treatment, and corrections. His research showed that it was just as important to enhance the attractiveness of the helper as to try to change the helpee. While many traditional approaches for troubled youth saw them as "perpetrators," Arnie embraced Kurt Lewin's interactionist approach: Behavior is a function of a person interacting with an environment, which Arnie called the "person-environment duet." If the person is to change, the ecology must be changed.

Finally, Arnie had little time for holy wars among behavioral, cognitive, and developmental perspectives. Instead, he sought to integrate wisdom from these diverse theories. With all of his behavioral expertise, he was among the first to recognize the modest potency of social skills training in isolation. Thus, in ART he added anger management and moral reasoning and designed interventions attuned to the ecology of children and youth. Employing many methods for many needs, he created powerful evidence-based interventions long before the notion was in style. ART evolved into the initial edition of *The Prepare Curriculum* in 1988, revised in 1999. Arnie realized that if we are to meet the needs of those we serve, strategies need to be prescriptive in nature. Thus Prepare provided additional resources to assist change agents. This Prepare Curriculum Implementation Guide provides practitioners with a practical outline for implementing these strategies, in a user friendly, evidence-based manner. In this spirit, those of us who follow in the footsteps of Arnold Goldstein continue the search for methods that create deep learning and enduring change.

LARRY K. BRENDTRO, PhD
STARR COMMONWEALTH INSTITUTE FOR TRAINING
ALBION, MICHIGAN

## References

Gibbs, J. C., Potter, G. B., & Goldstein, A. P. (1995). *The EQUIP Program: Teaching youth to think and act responsibly through a peer-helping approach.* Champaign, IL: Research Press.

Goldstein, A. P. (1988). *The Prepare Curriculum: Teaching prosocial competencies.* Champaign, IL: Research Press.

Goldstein, A. P. (1990). *Delinquents on delinquency.* Champaign, IL: Research Press.

Goldstein, A. P. (1999). *The Prepare Curriculum: Teaching prosocial competencies* (Rev. ed.). Champaign, IL: Research Press.

Goldstein, A. P., & Glick, B. (1987). *Aggression Replacement Training: A comprehensive intervention for aggressive youth.* Champaign, IL: Research Press.

# Preface

In September of 2001, at a meeting of practitioners from all over the world held in Malmo, Sweden, Arnold P. Goldstein made clear his charge: The strategies and techniques he described in *The Prepare Curriculum: Teaching Prosocial Competencies* (Goldstein, 1988, 1999) were just the beginning. He challenged all in attendance to continue to develop his ideas through their own work and to share best practices to continue to grow the Prepare Curriculum.

As described in the introduction to this book, contributed by Clive R. Hollin, the Prepare Curriculum includes coordinated psychoeducational courses designed to teach prosocial competencies to adolescents and younger children who struggle with various aspects of social and emotional behavior. The curriculum is still widely in use; however, Prepare methods have evolved over the years, resulting in many useful adaptations and expansions. Organizations and research groups formed to share ideas. The United States Center for Aggression Replacement Training ultimately developed into the organization as a worldwide network of researchers and practitioners known as ICART (International Center for Aggression Replacement Training), appointed by Arnold Goldstein with the aim of promoting quality control, further development, and continued dissemination of his programs. ICART evolved into PREPSEC (PRepare for Evidence-based Practice in Social Emotional Competency) International, a special interest organization designed to promote and expand Arnold P. Goldstein's combinations of programs for training in social competencies based on the Prepare Curriculum and other programs of a similar nature.

Likewise, this and other Prepare Curriculum Implementation Guides are intended to further Arnold Goldstein's original work—specifically, by describing and giving direction to the continued expansion of the Prepare methods. In conjunction with the original curriculum, the guides are designed to offer practitioners coherent, evidence-based approaches to enhancing the prosocial abilities of young people. We will be forever grateful to Dr. Goldstein and his contribution to the field of prevention and intervention and his humanistic approach to treating children and their families. We hope these guides will enhance the ability of motivated, skilled, and enthusiastic practitioners to put his effective methods to work.

MARK AMENDOLA      ROBERT OLIVER
PERSEUS HOUSE, INC.      PERSEUS HOUSE EDUCATION AND TREATMENT
ERIE, PENNSYLVANIA      ALTERNATIVES
ERIE, PENNSYLVANIA

# Acknowledgments

Social Perception Training has been tested in Norway by students of the postgraduate "Training in Social Competence" program throughout the past three years. Many of the examples in this book have been collected by these students. Thanks to all who have experienced the program and shared their experiences. A special thanks goes to Lisbeth Valgjord and Jan Arild Gundersen, who have had great impact on the final result by suggesting improvement and providing practical examples from work in the residential institution and school settings. We would also like to thank Frode Svartdal, Johannes Finne, Tutte Michell Olsen, and Eskil Domben at the Center for Social Competence at Diakonhjemmet University College and the board colleges from PREPSEC International for their fruitful discussions. A special thanks goes to Karen Steiner from Research Press for her thorough and skillful work with language and for bringing the manuscript into a logical structure.

# Introduction: About the Prepare Curriculum

*—Clive R. Hollin*

*The Prepare Curriculum*, developed and later revised by Arnold Goldstein (Goldstein, 1988, 1999), takes a psychoeducational approach to working with young people who experience difficulties with interpersonal relationships and prosocial behavior. Prepare is designed to provide practitioners, teachers, and therapists with a series of coordinated psychoeducational courses explicitly developed to teach an array of prosocial psychological competencies to adolescents and younger children who are deficient in such competencies. As Goldstein notes in the introduction to the 1999 edition:

> It seeks to teach empathy, which is interwoven into many of the modules, cooperation to the uncooperative, problem solving to those with inadequate decision-making skills, negotiating skills to the stubborn, anger control to the impulsive, altruism to the egocentric, group process to the isolated, stress management to the anxious, and social perceptiveness to the socially confused. (p. 1)

Prepare has its practice roots firmly in the tradition of skills training (Hollin & Trower, 1986a, 1986b) and, allied to social learning theory, to the application of cognitive-behavioral therapy to adolescent problems (Goldstein, Nensén, Daleflod, & Kalt, 2004). The techniques used in Prepare—including modeling, cognitive skills training, emotional control training, and problem-solving training—are traditional components of cognitive-behavioral interventions used to bring about change in cognitive, emotional, and behavioral skills. As these behavior change techniques are used in unison to bring about a range of changes, Prepare is an example of a multimodal program. A multimodal approach is in sympathy with the view that to bring about change in people's lives it is necessary to attend to multiple factors (Nietzel, Hasemann, & Lynam, 1999; Tate, Reppucci, & Mulvey, 1995). The effectiveness of multimodal programs such as Prepare with young people is supported in the literature (Hatcher & Hollin, 2005; Hollin & Palmer, 2006b; Lipsey & Wilson, 1998).

---

Clive R. Hollin is Professor of Psychology at the University of Leicester in England. His research lies in the interface between psychology and criminology, particularly with regard to the management and treatment of offenders.

1

Prepare also has foundations in an earlier program, described in the book *Aggression Replacement Training* (ART; Glick & Gibbs, 2011; Goldstein & Glick, 1987; Goldstein, Glick, & Gibbs, 1998). ART encompasses a tripartite approach, employing the three behavior change techniques of Skillstreaming, Anger Control Training, and Moral Reasoning. Whereas ART was designed for use with highly aggressive young people, Prepare incorporates a considerably wider spectrum of techniques aimed at the larger numbers of young people who have difficulties with prosocial behavior. Thus, Prepare may be used with young people who are moderately aggressive or who are socially isolated and withdrawn.

## PREPARE COURSES

The Prepare Curriculum consists of 10 courses that focus on the behaviors, cognitions, and emotions related to prosocial interaction. These courses target three areas: aggression, stress, and prejudice reduction. As shown in Table 1, the Prepare courses for aggression include the three original ART courses (Skillstreaming, Anger Control Training, and Moral Reasoning Training), with an additional course on Situational Perception Training. The courses that focus on stress are Recruiting Supportive Models, Stress Management Training, and Problem-Solving Training. Finally, the courses for prejudice reduction include Cooperation Training, Empathy Training, and Understanding and Using Groups.

## THEORETICAL BACKGROUND

Goldstein (1999) describes how several theoretical perspectives influenced both the original design and later refinement of the Prepare Curriculum. Acknowledging the importance of psychodynamic and client-centered theory approaches to helping people change, Goldstein is clear that social learning theory and skills training are the key influences of Prepare. Simply, social learning theory seeks to understand the complex interactions among an individual's thoughts, emotions, and actions within a given social context (Bandura, 1977b, 1986). In terms of practice, social learning theory is perhaps most closely allied with cognitive-behavioral methods, including skills training, traditionally much used with antisocial young people (Hollin, 1990). Furthermore, Goldstein's view of interpersonal problems is very much in sympathy with a social learning approach. For example, Goldstein (1994) described three levels in the physical ecology of aggression, all incorporating various levels of a person-environment interaction: "Macrolevel" refers to the analysis of aggression at a national or regional level, "mesolevel" to violence at the neighborhood level, and "microlevel" to violence found in settings such as the home and on the street.

The application of social learning theory is axiomatic with an approach to practice that sees the possibilities for change in both the social environment and the individual. At the level of work with the individual young person, practice is concerned with multimodal change that encompasses the individual's thoughts, emotions, and actions. As is evident from the curriculum, Prepare adopts a multimodal approach to change, with a clear emphasis on skills development. Indeed, the approach to skills development within Prepare is in keeping with the original social skills model described by Argyle and Kendon (1967). Argyle and Kendon described socially skilled behavior as consisting of three related components—namely, social perception, social cognition, and social performance. Social perception skills are evident in the ability to perceive and

**Table 1: Grouping of Prepare Curriculum Courses**

|  | AGGRESSION | STRESS | PREJUDICE REDUCTION |
|---|---|---|---|
| Behavioral | Skillstreaming<br><br>Situational Perception Training | Recruiting Supportive Models | Cooperation Training |
| Emotional | Anger Control Training | Stress Management Training | Empathy Training |
| Cognitive | Moral Reasoning Training | Problem-Solving Training | Understanding and Using Groups |

understand verbal and nonverbal social cues. Social cognition, as used in this context, is broadly analogous to social information processing and social problem solving. Social performance refers to the individual's own mastery of verbal and nonverbal behaviors. The socially able person will be able to use all three components of social skills in an integrated manner to function effectively with other people.

Newer research on brain development and the neurosciences also has had an impact on our understanding of social cognition and perception. Goleman's (2005) work with social intelligence assists with the development of best practice for social skills training. His discussion of the brain's design to be sociable provides a neural bridge that impacts learning. The more strongly we are connected with someone emotionally, the greater the potential for lasting change. So, just as prosocial relationships affect neurological connectedness by impacting the size and shape of synapses, negative relationships can have a toxic effect. These newer developments have important implications for evidence-based programs.

## RESEARCH OVERVIEW

If the theoretical and practical underpinnings of the Prepare Curriculum are sound, what is the evidence to suggest that some young people have specific difficulties in the areas addressed within Prepare? A body of research suggests that the three major targets of aggression, stress, and prejudice reduction within Prepare are aimed at appropriate aspects of young people's functioning with respect to their prosocial behavior. An overview of this evidence in support of the behavioral, emotional, or cognitive change for these three major targets is next provided.

### Behavior Focus

#### Situational Perception Training

Situational Perception Training is designed to develop the young person's social competence in applying the social skills learned in Skillstreaming. The purpose of Situational Perception Training is to show that in a social interaction, as well as in the other person's actions, situational, contextual factors are important to consider. The skill of accurately perceiving a person-situation interaction, rather than assuming, say, that another person is deliberately hostile, is an important element in developing social competence.

The skills to recognize, understand, and interpret situational cues are an essential part of effective interpersonal behavior (Argyle, 1983). However, some young people with interpersonal difficulties, including aggression, may have difficulties in both the selection and interpretation of social cues (e.g., Akhtar & Bradley, 1991; Lipton, McDonel, & McFall, 1987; Lösel, Bliesener, & Bender, 2007; McCown, Johnson, & Austin, 1986). The misperception of social cues may lead to misattribution of the actions of other people as hostile or threatening (Crick & Dodge, 1996). Misperception of the other people's intent will, in turn, influence the way in which the young person deals with a given social encounter. Thus, Situational Perception Training is intended to develop the young person's skills in accurately detecting and understanding the verbal and nonverbal nuances that are present within a social interaction. Situational Perception Training therefore focuses on the setting in which the interaction takes place, the purpose of the interaction, and the social relationship between those involved (Brown & Fraser, 1979). The learning that takes place with perception training augments the skill development associated with Skillstreaming, enhancing the closeness of the match between Prepare and the original social skills model (Argyle & Kendon, 1967). The closeness of the match between theory and practice increases the likelihood of a successful outcome. The expansion of the Prepare course is called Social Perception Training to reflect its more comprehensive nature.

## Skillstreaming

Skillstreaming is the development of skills, through the use of the techniques of modeling, instruction, practice, and feedback, to allow the young person to replace destructive behaviors with more constructive, prosocial alternative behaviors. Spence (1981a, 1981b) compared the social performance skills of young male offenders with those of matched nondelinquent controls. Spence reported differences in levels of nonverbal skills such that the delinquents were rated less favorably in terms of social skill, social anxiety, and employability. Ample evidence shows that skills training—incorporating modeling, role-play, and instructional feedback—can increase young people's social skills (Hollin & Palmer, 2001).

## Recruiting Supportive Models

The Prepare course on recruiting supportive models aims to help young people to recognize, recruit, and maintain a prosocial support group. Goldstein's (2004a, 2004b) evaluation of the three original ART courses concludes that participation of the individual's significant other(s) in the courses is likely further to improve their success. The extension of the Prepare course Recruiting Supportive Models is *Family TIES* (Teaching in Essential Skills; Calame & Parker, 2013), which incorporates the family as the main support system.

## Cooperation Training

The Prepare Curriculum originally involved two broad approaches designed to increase cooperative behavior: cooperative learning and cooperative gaming. The course offered numerous exercises, organized by age group, to enhance prosocial and achievement behaviors.

Johnson, Johnson, and Stanne (2000) conducted a meta-analysis of 158 studies of cooperative learning strategies. They reported that the research clearly presents evidence that cooperative learning produces positive achievement results. Brown and Ciuffetelli (2009) highlight five basic and essential elements of cooperative learning: (a) positive interdependence; (b) face-to-face promotive interaction; (c) individual accountability; (d) social skills; and (e) group processing. Other positive outcomes of cooperative learning are increased self- and co-regulation leading to better problem solving (DiDonato, 2013).

Movement training utilizes cooperative activities and games to further enhance learning and retention of the skills taught to youth who participate in the Prepare series groups. Movement training incorporates physical movements that will stimulate and prepare the brain for learning. Ratey (2008) describes movement and exercise as "Miracle-Gro" for the brain, greatly enhancing self-awareness, self-esteem, and social skills. The typical child's attention span is reported to be three to five minutes per year of the child's age (Schmitt, 1999). A decrease in attention is exacerbated by inactivity. Movement can be used before, during, and after group participation to increase attention and enhance learning.

## Emotion Focus

### Anger Control Training

Anger Control Training involves the application of anger management techniques to previously assessed triggers for the young person's anger. Thus, this course aims to improve the young person's control over anger by developing a self-awareness of internal anger cues, increasing self-instructional skills, facilitating the use of coping strategies and social problem-solving skills, and increasing social skills.

Anger, particularly dysfunctional anger, is the emotional state most frequently associated with aggressive behavior (Davey, Day, & Howells, 2005), although not all violent conduct is associated with anger. Anger is seen to be dysfunctional when it has a negative consequence either for the individual, as seen with poor physical and mental health, or for other people (Swaffer & Hollin, 2000, 2001). The most influential theory of anger was formulated by Novaco (1975, 2007), in which anger is understood to be a subjective emotional state involving both physiological and cognitive activity, but clearly related to environmental circumstances.

Following Novaco's theory, the experience of anger is triggered by some environmental event, typically the individual's perception of the words and actions of another person. Novaco and Welsh (1989) identified various styles of perception and information processing that are typical of individuals who are prone to anger. These styles include the tendency to see hostility and provocation in the words and actions of other people and to make attribution errors in perceiving one's own behavior as situationally determined by the behavior of others, as explained by their negative personality.

The individual's misperception of a situation may prompt distinct patterns of physiological and cognitive arousal. The physiological correlates of anger are typically a rise in body temperature, perspiration and muscular tension and increased cardiovascular activity. The cognitive processes begin with the individual's labeling the emotional state as anger and then continue with the intensification of the information-processing biases as the situation unfolds. Finally, the shift from anger to violent behavior is related to the disinhibition of internal control through, for example, high levels of physiological arousal or the effects of drugs.

Anger control training in various forms is now widely used across a range of populations, including young people, with a strong supporting research base (Hollin & Bloxsom, 2007).

## Stress Management Training

Stress Management Training recognizes that stressful life events may have negative effects on young people. The development of stress management skills is achieved through the application of such techniques as progressive relaxation training, meditation, controlled breathing, and physical exercise, as well as through reflective exercises looking at how to deal with personally stressful life events.

As is the case with anger, stress and anxiety can be both functional and dysfunctional. Childhood and adolescence present a myriad of changing life events that are naturally stressful for the developing young adult (Frydenberg, 1997). The Stress Management Training course in Prepare aims to help individuals regulate their stress so that it does not affect their ability to use their prosocial skills effectively. The tendency of adolescents to be peer-conscious can make some young people particularly susceptible to social stressors. The experience of stress, in turn, may interfere with the young person's ability to perform well in some social interactions.

## Empathy Training

Empathy Training encourages young people to reflect upon other people's feelings and to increase awareness that the feelings of other people may be different from their own. The basis of this training lies in the view that if an individual has the capacity to empathize, then he or she is less likely to misperceive hostile intent in the actions of other people. Increasing empathy may reduce the likelihood of the young person's being aggressive toward others.

The ability to appreciate another person's emotional state is a key component of prosocial behavior. Goldstein (2004a) suggests that empathy and aggression cannot coexist, given that an empathic state will inhibit an aggressive one. It follows, therefore, that increasing a young person's capacity for empathy may reduce the likelihood of the young person's displaying hostility and aggression to other people.

A distinction is made in the literature between affective empathy and cognitive empathy. Affective empathy is seen in the emotions we experience in response to another person's situation. Cognitive empathy is our intellectual understanding of how another person feels. The research literature suggests a relationship between low empathy and offending (Miller & Eisenberg, 1988). Jolliffe and Farrington (2007) found a relationship between low cognitive and affective empathy and offending. However, Jolliffe and Farrington also reported that the relationship was more consistent in males than in females and was moderated by the level of the young person's intelligence and socioeconomic status. These studies provide support for the inclusion of empathy training as an integral part of Prepare.

## Cognitive Focus

### Moral Reasoning Training

Moral Reasoning Training is intended to resolve maturational delays with respect to moral reasoning and any associated egocentric bias. This aspect of Prepare includes enhancement of moral reasoning, alongside social perspective-taking skills, using the techniques of self-instruction training, social problem-solving skills training, and guided peer group social decision making.

The importance of moral development in socialization is made clear in several influential theories (Kohlberg, 1978; Piaget, 1932). In particular, Kohlberg's theory is concerned with the development of antisocial behavior. Kohlberg, like Piaget, argues that as the child grows older moral reasoning follows a developmental sequence in line with the child's age. Kohlberg describes three levels of moral development, with two stages at each level. At the lower stages, moral reasoning is concrete in orientation. Reasoning becomes more abstract at the higher stages, involving concepts such as justice and rights.

Kohlberg suggests that antisocial behavior is associated with a delay in the development of moral reasoning that results in weak internal control over behavior. The generally accepted position, reinforced by the major reviews, is that delinquents typically show immature, hedonistic, and self-centered moral functioning when compared with their nondelinquent peers (Nelson, Smith, & Dodd, 1990; Palmer, 2003; Stams et al., 2006).

However, as Gibbs (1993) points out, moral reasoning should be considered alongside other aspects of cognition, particularly social information processing, particularly with regard to cognitive distortions (Gibbs, 1993; Goldstein et al., 1998). Cognitive distortions directly support the attitudes consistent with sociomoral developmental delay and reduce cognitive dissonance. Thus, an example of self-centered moral reasoning would be "If I want it, I take it." Gibbs terms this type of reasoning a primary distortion. Primary distortions are sustained by secondary distortions: Secondary distortions supporting "I want it, I take it" might be blaming victims for the offense or biased interpretations of one's own behavior. The successful use of Moral Reasoning Training with aggressive populations has been reported in the literature (Gibbs, 1996; Gibbs, Potter, & Goldstein, 1995).

### Problem-Solving Training

Problem-Solving Training is included because the young person's problem-solving ability affects how successfully he or she may learn and apply other Prepare skills in real life. Thus, Problem-Solving Training helps the young person develop skills and abilities in defining a problem, identifying potential solutions, selecting the optimal solution, and evaluating the effectiveness of the chosen strategy.

Following perception and understanding of other people's behavior, the young person must choose a suitable behavioral response. The process of decision making in the context of a social interaction requires the young person to problem-solve—that is, to think of potential courses of action, to consider the alternatives and their likely consequences, and to plan toward accomplishing the intended outcome (McGuire, 2005). Some young people may experience difficulties in social problem solving. For example, both female and male young offenders typically employ a more limited range of alternatives to solve interpersonal problems and rely more on verbal and physical aggression than do nondelinquents (Hollin & Palmer, 2006a; Palmer & Hollin, 1999; Ward & McFall, 1986). A body of research that supports the effectiveness of problem-solving training with young people (Lösel & Beelmann, 2005).

## Understanding and Using Groups

As Goldstein (1999) points out, "Group processes are an exceedingly important influence upon the daily lives of many adolescents and younger children" (p. 737). The Prepare course on groups encompasses discussion of the nature, dynamics, problems, and opportunities in groups. In addition to providing a conceptual context, the course describes numerous experiential opportunities to help youth understand and use groups to prosocial advantage.

Groups develop through four stages: forming, storming, norming, and performing (Tuckman, 1965; Tuckman & Jensen, 1977). At the forming stage, even though members may not know each other very well, it is important to set boundaries and clear parameters for the operation of the group. Safety is clearly the priority, for if there is no safety, there is no growth. When groups are forming, the facilitators provide support and guidance to establish a climate of psychological and emotional safety. Facilitators also should be keenly aware of any negative influences in the group and any bullying behavior that may be unsafe and/or counterproductive to the goals of the group.

In the second stage, storming, members will test limits to determine whether the group is safe. Individuals may push boundaries and break commitments that they made in the initial session. It is the role and responsibility of facilitators to correct and/or address such behavior. If facilitators and members fail to enforce and comply with norms, the safety and growth of the group will be impaired.

During the third stage, norming, relationships develop, and, as trust increases, members become more willing to take risks (Amidon, Roth, & Greenberg, 1991). The group should begin to work together to problem-solve, resolve conflict, and share personal values. Because adolescents are constantly attempting to discover their identity and role in relation to others, their interaction with one another, if positive, will assist in crystallizing this identity and role. Also during this stage, we begin to see prosocial coaching occur from peer to peer. When this transpires, our experience has been that group members begin to internalize and learn skills at a deeper level.

In the more advanced performing stage, we begin to see the group functioning at its highest level. Facilitators' roles are to ease transitions and provide support to the group. Trust is at its highest level, and we also see peers exhibit empathic responses to one another. During this time, higher risk engagement and activities are possible, with facilitators remaining intensely aware of any negative environmental influences.

When delivered with fidelity, psychoeducational groups can help increase self-awareness, build healthy relationships, and improve interpersonal connections. This therapeutic environment also assists with competency development and skill building, which encourage appropriate expression of emotion, minimizing the negative and maximizing the positive. Processing group experiences also increases self-awareness, self-disclosure, healthy boundaries, and improved relationships (Thompson & White, 2010).

We have found through our practical application of the Prepare Curriculum that the development of group process is impacted by the skill level of the facilitator and engagement of the participants. When groups are functioning at their highest level, there is mutual benefit to a larger number of participants, and we see proficient levels of skill demonstrated in real-life situations.

## CONCLUSION

Some young people experience difficulties as they grow older in developing and using prosocial skills. These difficulties are obviously not a characteristic of all young people, who form a heterogeneous population with an accordingly broad span of social ability (Veneziano & Veneziano, 1988). Nonetheless, for those young people who do experience such problems, attention to the development of prosocial competencies may help in reducing antisocial behavior and moving them toward a more rewarding social life.

# PART 1

# Theoretical Foundation and Program Overview

# THEORETICAL FOUNDATION

A large body of evidence suggests a possible causal link between lack of prosocial competence and factors such as loneliness (Jones, Hobbs, & Hockenbury, 1982), depression (Tse & Bond, 2004), bullying and aggression (DeRosier, 2004), and drug and alcohol abuse (Gaffney, Thorpe, Young, Collett, & Occhipinti, 1998). A causal connection has also been shown between children's ability to forge friendships and the degree of lifelong mental problems (Hay, Payne, & Chadwick, 2004). Furthermore, a correlation has been established between lack of social skills and behavioral problems in persons with autism (Njardvik, Matson, & Cherry, 1999) and mental retardation (Patel, 2004). From this perspective, the growing emphasis on programs for training prosocial competence in both schools and institutions has been very positive.

Social interaction may be seen as a process involving certain steps: attention, interpretation, response generation, and response evaluation. This view of social interaction corresponds to the content in Dodge's social information processing theory, which will be discussed in more detail later in this book. In general, children and young people with behavioral problems have, for various reasons, problems with one or more of these steps (Foster & Crain, 2002). Weiss, Dodge, Bates, and Pettit (1992) found that children with difficulties in these abilities were strongly overrepresented in cases of behavioral problems in kindergarten. In Social Perception Training (SPT) sessions, the focus is specifically on the interpretation of situations and the intentions of the other. A precise interpretation includes factors such as interpreting the other's feelings, assessment of underlying events, understanding of unwritten laws and rules, awareness of other forms of cultural expression, and assessment of others' intentions. Each session in SPT focuses on one of these aspects so participants gradually expand their basis for accurate interpretation. In each session, a number of steps are carried out, including the generation of alternative courses of action based on both interpretation and understanding of how the alternative chosen is experienced from the other's point of view and awareness of the consequences an action will have both for self and other.

Although these factors (attention, interpretation, response generation, and response evaluation) in our view make up the core of the concept of social competence, the following discussion will describe and define some additional characteristics of the concept that may provide background useful in implementing SPT.

## What Is Prosocial Competence?

Having reviewed definitions by several authors (Bellack, Mueser, Gingerich, & Agresta, 1997; Goldstein, 1999; O'Donohue & Krasner, 1995; Schlundt & McFall, 1985), we emphasize the following four characteristics.

### Variety of Skills

Prosocial competence is not a single skill, but a variety of relational skills that must be adapted to different social contexts (Schlundt & McFall, 1985). The concept of social skills denotes specific behavioral sequences that a person must master to be able to behave competently in social contexts. Goldstein's 50 social skills for adolescents (Goldstein & McGinnis, 1997; McGinnis, 2012a) and Ellen McGinnis's 60 social skills for school-age children (McGinnis, 2012b; McGinnis & Goldstein, 1997) are examples of this. These skills, part of the Skillstreaming curricula, are divided into action sequences or steps that involve both cognitive reasoning and practical performance. The skills must be adapted to the situation at hand and the culture in which the social interaction takes place, as well as to the responses given by the partners in such situations. Matching these requirements requires mastering a large number of subresponses, or microskills. A simple interaction such as shaking hands is thus evaluated not only according to whether the steps were actually carried out, but also according to factors such as intensity (strength of handshake and of voice, vocal pitch, and distance between the parties), duration (duration of handshake and of eye contact), and frequency (how often handshaking takes place). All of these dimensions can be understood on the basis of a continuum from too little/too weak to too much/too strong.

Even if an individual technically masters most of the social skills, prosocial competence also requires a good deal of adaptation in order to choose the skills that are most relevant to the situation. Cognitive reasoning, in the form of observing and interpreting social situations, comprehending roles, developing strategies for solving problems, and being able to adapt one's own behavior to the signals of one's interpersonal partner (matching), is of major importance. This is what is termed *contextual modeling* (Bandura, 1977b, 2006).

In the two editions of *The Prepare Curriculum*, Goldstein (1988, 1999) encouraged the reader to differentiate between social skill and social competence. Social skill was defined as the ability to *perform* or execute specific interpersonal behaviors, as described in the chapters on Skillstreaming, Anger Control Training, Moral Reasoning Training, and Cooperation Training. Social competence is construed as an evaluative ability required to judge the appropriateness and need for specific social skills in specific social contexts or situations. Like Schlundt and McFall (1985), Goldstein defined social competence as an ability an individual uses to perceive when, where, and how to perform a variety of skills that are demanded in all social encounters.

### Empathic or Moral Dimension

Prosocial competence also has an empathic or moral dimension. Phillips (1985) stresses that prosocial competence is not simply a one-sided means of reaching one's own goals, but a mutual process whereby the person behaves in a way that satisfies his or her own rights, needs, goals, or obligations while the person one is relating to (referred to as the partner or partners) is satisfied correspondingly. A salesperson who is good at getting people to buy things they don't need, or someone who seduces others solely for self-gratification before dumping them, is not an example of prosocial competence according to the criteria set here (O'Donohue & Krasner, 1995). This dimension is addressed directly in the Moral Reasoning Training part of Prepare, but implications of cognitive distortions and immoral ways of reasoning must also be considered in SPT.

### Positive Influence and Adherence to Norms

Prosocial competence means having a positive influence on one's social network and behaving in accordance with the rules and norms of one's culture (Schlundt & McFall, 1985). Two people cooperating to smuggle drugs do not demonstrate prosocial competence according to this definition. An extension of this perspective indicates that each situation is an interaction between situational and personal demands and the resources in the situation and within the person. This idea is expressed graphically in Figure 1.

## Figure 1: Interaction of Demands and Resources

Situational demands ⟷ Personal resources

Situational resources ⟷ Personal demands

*Situational demands* (understood also as possibilities) may be communicated in the form of explicit rules or regulations, as may be experienced in official settings such as courts, social services, police stations, schools, and so on. They may be communicated in the form of written or spoken instructions and may be highly specific. We term such demands *explicit* because they specify what behavior is required and when it is to be performed. Thus explicit demands prescribe and proscribe specific actions and behaviors for persons, groups, and organizations in specific or more general contexts. Demands also may be communicated more implicitly, as is the case in the vast majority of daily social interactions. *Implicit* demands are conveyed through a gamut of nonverbal and verbal behavior, vocal and nonvocal expressions, hints, gestures and so on. The most pervasive and potentially useful way of conveying these demands is by observing the actions of other participants in social situations as models for action.

*Personal demands* or possibilities in situations express the legal rights and considerations that one person can expect in a specific situation. These can be divided into formal demands (as expressed in laws and regulations) and informal demands (expectations of respect for cultural background and consideration of personal abilities).

*Situational resources* are resources available in the situation. Most often and most importantly, this will mean other people in the situation, but resources also include informational resources, such as posters, books, pamphlets, and computers. It also may be possible for individuals to make use of mobile phones or personal computers to enlist the aid of other persons outside a situation, such as experts, counselors, or friends.

*Personal resources* signify the learning history of actors in social situations and their skills in performing required actions. It also refers to reflexive competence, where the person involved demonstrates an ability to decide that he or she has adequate skills with which to act effectively in the situation.

The arrows in Figure 1 indicate the dynamic connection between demands and resources. There must be concordance between the demands in a situation and the resources of the individual. Increasing social competence and thereby increasing personal resources will contribute to meeting the explicit and implicit demands in any given situation. Personal abilities or cultural background of the individual will also contribute to a balance between resources and demands.

### Appropriateness to the Situation

Prosocial competence also entails that one is capable of exercising the social skill that is appropriate to the situation at hand. The skill may have been learned, but due to lack of knowledge or anxiety about which skill is appropriate in the specific situation, an individual may be hampered in applying the skill. Bandura (1977a) argues that a person's faith in his or her own abilities is equally and sometimes more important than the actual performance of social skills in a given social situation. High arousal of emotions such as anger may activate old, counterproductive strategies for reacting to the daily challenges of social life. Further examples of the debilitating effects of emotional arousal are when persons exhibit anxiety prior to or while performing social skills. They may focus on effects of their anxiety such as rapid heartbeat, sweating, or tremors and retreat from the situation to avoid prolonging the experience or risking that the effects may worsen. These reactions can result in both positive and negative reinforcement associated with the use of the skill and lead to the person's being less inclined to perform that skill later on (O'Donohue & Krasner, 1995).

଼ଡ଼ଔ

Of course, a prerequisite for prosocial performance is that the person have the social skills in his or her repertoire in order to perform them.

Based on the factors just discussed, we define prosocial competence as follows:

> A person exhibits pro-social competence when (i) he/she, in given social situations and with great probability, achieves personal, joint and common goals in ways that preserve his/her own rights and those of the partner(s), (ii) satisfies explicit rules of his/her culture and society and meets implicit standards of behavior. (Gundersen & moynahan, 2003, p. 296)

The aim of prosocial competence training, including Social Perception Training, is thus to develop the ability to perceive and understand the intentions of partners, be familiar with the implicitly and explicitly expressed rules that apply to the situation, have a set of relevant skills that can be applied, and choose those that yield a positive result for both oneself and one's partner.

Goldstein was very aware of the importance of the interaction between the individual and the environment, as demonstrated in his citation of the following extract:

> Adequate social performance not only requires a repertoire of response skills, but knowledge about when and how these responses should be applied. Application of this knowledge, in turn, depends upon the ability to accurately "read" the social environment, determine the particular norms and conventions operating at the moment, and to understand the message being sent and the particular emotions and intentions guiding the behavior of the interpersonal partner. . . . The literature on social perception. . . has important implications for social skills training. In the past, such training has primarily focused on response capability. Information about when and where to apply new responses has only been provided as an incidental part of treatment. (Morrison & Bellack, 1981, as cited in Goldstein, 1994, p. 70)

Although several cognitive elements are incorporated into Goldstein's (1999) social skills training program, as exemplified by the use of self-talk ("bubble talk") and skill steps such as choosing the right time and place, the program says nothing about *how* to choose the right time and place. This is one of the background factors for Goldstein's proposal of the Situational Perception Training course, which we now have developed into our Social Perception Training program.

## Rationale for Training Social Perception

A correct perception of various social situations is integrated to a greater or lesser extent into all the different Prepare courses. We have mentioned "the right time and place" in the social skills program, but understanding the feelings of others in the social skills course and in the empathy course is an example of actual situational perception training. The step "defining the problem" as used in the Problem-Solving Program is also social perception training, as is defining the moral dilemma in Moral Reasoning and identifying triggers and setting events in Anger Control Training. Thus one can say that working thoroughly with most of the components in Prepare, including efforts to achieve generalization, will almost certainly also ensure social perception training. In particular, working with Skillstreaming role-plays will contribute to a more profound understanding of the different perspectives that may be considered in specific social settings. Regardless of an individual's ability to perform different social responses, he or she cannot perform effectively without the ability to recognize, understand, and interpret interpersonal cues. The socially skillful individual attends to partner(s), analyzes the situation, and knows when, where, and how to structure his or her response. This combination of attention, analysis, and knowledge is generally referred to as social perception (Bellack, Mueser, Gingerich, & Agresta, 2004).

The purpose of SPT is to help participants correctly interpret the rules and intentions that apply in a given social context. The term *context* has temporal, physical, and social characteristics, which must be perceived in order to carry out or to refrain from carrying out actions to participate effectively.

In grouping the Prepare Curriculum courses, Goldstein (2004) suggests that Situational Perception Training should be a part of the course addressing anger problems, together with Skillstreaming, Anger Control Training, and Moral Reasoning Training, together referred to as Aggression Replacement Training, or ART. The strong connection between aggression and biases in interpreting social cues makes such training very important in anger management. There is no doubt a strong connection between anger problems in general and faulty attributions of the other person's intent in the situation (see Crick & Dodge, 1996; Dodge, 2006). A body of evidence also suggests that individuals with higher levels of overall aggression generally misidentify emotions from facial expressions (McCown, Johnson, & Austin, 1986) and more specifically inaccurately identify anger (Hall, 2006). Novaco and Welsh (1989) point to five typical features found in persons with behavioral disorders that may influence their way of perceiving situations:

1. *Attention disorder* (i.e., a tendency in persons disposed to anger to perceive the behavior of others as hostile and inflammatory).
2. *Mixed perception* (i.e., quickly resorting to aggression because it works in other situations).
3. *Attribution disorder* (i.e., blaming one's own aggressive behavior on circumstances in the situation, while explaining aggression in someone else as a permanent characteristic in that person).

4. *False consensus* (i.e., the tendency to believe that more people agree with one's views than is actually the case. This in turn impedes the ability to consider the other person's perspective).

5. *Cognitive lock* (i.e., if the person has initially assessed the situation in a particular way, the tendency to be locked into that perception, even if strong evidence emerges to indicate the opposite; see also Hollin, 2004).

Anger in itself can also influence the cognitive processes of perceived situations; thus anger can add fuel to perceiving aggressive actions as right: "You have made me angry; it is reasonable that I become aggressive." In this way, anger can disturb the cognitive processes that we use to understand the actual situation. It has also been suggested that objects and situations that can be connected with aggression also can influence the perception of the situation and become a setting event for more aggression. Examples of this are the availability of weapons (Carlson, Marcus-Newhall, & Miller, 1990) and standing in taxi queues (Goldstein, Glick, Carthan, & Blancero, 1994). It is also well known that anger resulting from earlier quarrels or generated by watching films or sports can be maintained over time and transferred to other situations or persons who are not responsible for the initial anger activation, thus becoming a part of the new perception (see Marcus-Newhall, Pedersen, Carlson, & Miller, 2000). Other factors that may influence the perception of situations involve attitudes (e.g., positive attitudes about aggression toward specific groups), values (e.g., social sets with strong codes for respect), personal goals (e.g., of being rich or being feared), or drug abuse. Physical conditions such as experiencing a headache or a lack of sleep can also distort the perception of the situation. Environmental conditions such as extreme heat, continual rain, or high humidity may also play a part in disturbing or perturbing our perception of social situations. In the SPT program, these factors are directly addressed in Session 5, "Setting Events."

Goldstein (1988) presents a long list of other possible sources of misunderstanding, including age, education, socioeconomic status, the perceiver's affective state (especially anxiety), degree of self-confidence, involvement in the situation, and threat level. Current research confirms these factors as important in influencing how situations are perceived (for more studies, see, for example, Chang, D'Zurilla, & Sanna, 2004). An especially important factor in understanding social misperception is the cultural aspect. Goldstein (1988) explains:

> We believe it is useful to describe the behavior of the perceiver (i.e., the individual entering into and needing to decode the situation) as being potentially cross-cultural in nature. To be sure, this term is typically reserved for encounters between persons of different nations, geographical entities, ethnic background, and so forth. However, we believe that the cross-cultural misperceptions, miscommunications, misunderstandings and faulty interpretations described here are every bit as operative. (p. 219)

Goldstein therefore included the work of the "Culture Assimilator" in Prepare's Situational Perception Training. Albert, the method's creator, makes the following comments:

When persons with different subjective cultures interact, their assumptions about, and interpretations of, particular behaviors may differ markedly. These assumptions and interpretations can be viewed in terms of attributions a person makes. Attributions are inferences about the causes of behavior. For example, a compliment can be seen as an attempt to manipulate, help can be interpreted as an attempt to demean, a gift can be seen as a bribe and so on.

Discrepancies in attributions may result in misunderstandings, low interpersonal attraction, rejection, and even conflict. Such discrepancies are more likely to occur when two individuals belong to different cultures because of the differences in norms, roles, attitudes, and values between the two cultures. One of the major aims of intercultural training is to help individuals understand the perspectives of another culture and to teach them about the other's subjective culture. (Albert, 1983, pp. 187–188)

We can conclude by stating that the situation-specific characteristics most important to identify are explicit and implicit expressed demands, roles, expectations and goals for the various players; cultural differences; emotional expressions; and setting events. Training should help participants to look for, question, and then analyze these factors before and while taking appropriate and effective action.

## Interpretation of Social Situations

When training in social perception, it is important to put the different factors associated with interpretation and misinterpretation of social situations deduced from research into a system that ensures that they are emphasized and utilized in overcoming the participants' difficulties in social interaction. Goldstein's (2004) position when describing the dimensions of accurate social perceptiveness responds to the leads provided by Brown and Fraser (1979): (a) the *setting* of the interaction and its associated rules and norms (b) the *purpose* of the interaction and its goals, tasks, and topics; and (c) the *relationship* of the participants, their roles, responsibilities, expectations, and group membership.

They propose a division of social perception skills into five general categories: precise observation/listening, identifying emotions, clarification, relevance, and timing. These categories are also relevant for people with aggression problems. *Precise observation, including listening,* is a crucial part of understanding a social situation. High arousal of emotions, intrusion of one's own problems, and other disturbances may result in distortion in understanding what is actually happening in the situation. Participants may fail to observe the behavior of partners and thus lose valuable information on which they may base their understanding and thus their subsequent actions. The first step in SPT is therefore to make the initial appraisal of a social situation subject to an agreement as to what actually happened in the situation.

A key factor for understanding a social situation is accurately *identifying emotions.* As previously described, many persons with behavioral problems lack skills in discrimination of emotional states and misinterpret situations. Understanding the underlying emotion connected to a verbal utterance can be of critical importance when determining an appropriate response. Understanding of emotion is also an important aspect of

SPT. A possible disadvantage in using discussion of written material (e.g., past events, stories, and role-plays) in training might be that the portrayal and subsequent clarification of emotions may be reduced. Role-playing of real-life situations can to a greater degree emphasize the role of emotions in affecting the actions of partners. Whether the participant(s) have missed valuable information or not, a situation may need *clarification* to prevent insecurity or confusion. Clarification can consist of asking for new information. Discrepancies between spoken words and body language may need to be cleared up. The more skilled the person is in interpreting situational norms and rules and the purpose and the relationship of the interpersonal partner, the less clarification is needed. Some of these variables can be clarified by asking the other person, but sometimes, especially in potential conflict situations, such questions can be ill-timed. A key aspect of SPT is therefore to clarify and prioritize the most important variables that influence common relevant situations, enabling participants to choose and use skills in real-life situations.

As Bellack and colleagues (2004) point out, to be appropriate, a response must be *relevant* to the interaction as a whole and to the immediately preceding communication. This involves either choosing or responding to a topic appropriate to the situation and matching the emotional state of the interpersonal partner. Both recognizing and adapting to the partner's emotion is in itself an important part of empathic behavior in general.

A person may have the necessary social skills in his or her repertoire but fail to perform these at appropriate points or with appropriate latency in the interaction. Bellack and colleagues (2004) describe this as *timing*. Social interactions are characterized by rapid movement between exchanges and silence. Without knowing the situational cues that indicate the right time and place to interact with other persons, a person runs great risk of creating irritation or anger. A connection exists between understanding underlying hidden social rules and lack of timing. Nowicki and Duke (1992) indicate that a high percentage of violent criminals have a learning disability called *dyssemia*. People with this condition fail to follow underlying hidden rules, intrude into others' personal space, and fail to follow or match the rhythm of others.

During their work, SPT facilitators must be aware of these aspects of the social exchange and ensure that they form part of the discussion during the sessions.

## Social Information Processing Theory and Social Perception Training

The structure of SPT is influenced by the social information processing theory formulated by Crick and Dodge (1996), with the inclusion of emotions (Lemerise & Arsenio, 2000) and morality (Arsenio & Lemerise, 2004). Based on this model, we view the reaction of children and young people to a problematic social situation as a function of cognitive, moral, and emotional processing through a five-step process (see also Gundersen, 2010).

All the aspects next discussed are included to a greater or lesser extent in the structure of the SPT program, and facilitators can emphasize different aspects depending on the capacity and needs of the participants.

### Encoding of Cues

Through this process, we observe relevant stimuli and recognize (decode) them in a way that gives them meaning. We draw on past experience and internalized systems for sorting new information. We often focus on special signals relevant to our interests and previous experiences. Children and young people with behavioral problems will often focus on negative elements in ambiguous situations while largely ignoring the emotional expressions, intentions, or content of the other person's action (Crick & Dodge, 1994). Among other factors that play a part are the mood the person is in (setting events), whether a moral evaluation of the situation is involved, and the person's attentive ability.

## Interpretation of Social Signals

Each individual has his or her own patterns of attribution, or ways to cognitively understand what is happening. A variety of relevant factors influence this process, including cultural understanding, interpretation of intention, the emotions of both receiver and transmitter of the message, sense of fairness, and whether the interpretation is mainly based on verbal or nonverbal signals. If a person in an ambiguous situation perceives the action as hostile, this will have a considerable influence on how the subsequent interaction develops. The tendency for people with behavioral problems to perceive others' actions as hostile in ambiguous situations is consistent across different patterns of aggression and just as apparent as other perceptual problems, such as lack of attention and hyperactivity (Waldman, 1996).

In relation to fairness and morality, Arsenio and Lemerise (2004) present the following example: There is a line at a drinking fountain, and a student sneaks in the line. Two other students both think that this action is not fair, but one of them may see this from the perspective that "he wants to be mean/he's showing off," whereas the other views it more as a breach of school rules. Yet other students may see the incident as "someone who's very thirsty" and think that we should be able to make exceptions to rules.

## Clarification of Goals

Goals can be categorized as internal (e.g., to remain in a good mood or to avoid embarrassment) or external (e.g., to assert oneself or win a competition) and as prosocial or antisocial. Socially competent children typically select goals that preserve friendships, such as playing together or cooperating, while antisocial children choose more instrumental goals, such as beating others at a game or taking back the place somebody else took.

## Generating Alternative Actions

The greater one's repertoire of alternative actions, the greater the chances of finding competent strategies as a means of avoiding trouble. Children and young people with behavioral problems generally have fewer alternative actions (Palmer & Hollin, 1996) and often choose such patterns as attacking or fleeing. As alternative actions are generated, they are evaluated according to their suitability for the situation. It turns out that if a person has time to reflect, he or she not only finds more alternative actions, but also chooses more prosocial and less aggressive ones.

## Response Decision

The choice of response is also influenced by a number of factors. The first is an assessment of the action according to moral values. Is the action perceived to be fair? The values are related to one's way of moral reasoning and to whether the person legitimizes antisocial behavior through the use of cognitive distortions. Another factor is whether a person is comfortable with the action. If a child is to carry out a specific action, the child must believe he or she is capable of it. Such a basic belief in one's own efficacy (Bandura, 1977a) will increase the probability that the child will choose the action. While most children will feel comfortable choosing a constructive, verbal response in answer to a frustrating or ambiguous social situation, less well-adjusted children may feel more comfortable responding aggressively. A third factor influencing the choice of response is the expected result of the action. Some children will be keen to maintain friendship, whereas others may be more concerned about maintaining their own position or "getting respect." Children with behavioral problems seem to have a tendency to expect a more positive outcome from aggression than do other children. Cultural/environmental differences as to what generates respect and the attitude toward aggression will obviously also play a large part in choice of reaction pattern (Nisbett & Cohen, 1996).

### Behavioral Enactment and Peer Evaluation

After the action itself, the person receives feedback both from his or her interaction partner(s) and his or her own assessment of the impact of the action. An important factor here is that there is a greater tendency to learn from the short-term consequences than from the long-term ones. Aggressive behavior thus tends to be reinforced because it often has a more immediate consequence.

ℰᗡᏹᏒ

The time span from when we receive an external stimulus from another person until we respond is usually very short, and we mostly make use of automatic thoughts and actions. The goal of the SPT program is to increase participants' ability to interpret social situations through increased understanding of the processes that take place in the various steps between stimulus and response. In this way, they can choose their response on the basis of a broader understanding and thereby increase their potential to generate more prosocial alternatives in stressful situations.

Crick and Dodge's (1994) model primarily describes the process between stimulus and response. In reality, interaction consists of a number of response exchanges, where one party's reactions represent a new stimulus for the other party. To illustrate this, we can take the example in Figure 2.

This is an example of a very rapid interaction that involves setting events or background variables (e.g., a person is more vulnerable to react negatively to stimuli on some occasions than on others (Ruth had a stressful day). It also involves emotions (Eivind did not see that Ruth was stressed and thought of his own needs for food and getting to training), unclear intentions (Does Ruth want to convey that she has had a bad day or that she will leave Eivind if he doesn't change?), and other factors. It is most likely that a small change in Ruth's husband's behavior in the form of better understanding of the background variables or a more direct ego message from Ruth at the next stage would prevent any serious conflict. The earlier one or both parties break this spiral of aggression, the easier it will be to reach constructive solutions instead of generating an even tougher conflict.

## PROGRAM OVERVIEW

Many of the Prepare courses use methods grounded in what has been termed *observational learning*. Observational learning, also termed *vicarious learning* (see Bandura,

## Figure 2: Response Exchanges in Interaction

Ruth has been home all day. A lot of things have gone wrong, and she hasn't done much of the cleaning and cooking she'd planned. Ruth's husband, Eivind, comes home.

Eivind walks toward the kitchen and asks, "Is the food ready?"

Ruth answers, annoyed, "You just presume that I'll do all the cooking while you live like a king."

Eivind looks sour and says, irritated, "I only asked about dinner. I'm in a hurry— you know I have training on Mondays. You've been home all day."

"It's always that training, isn't it? Now it's about time you did some housework, too. I'm not going to spend the rest of my life being your maid."

1977b) involves using a technique in which observers learn how to perform behaviors by watching the performance of others. These others are called *models* and are usually more proficient in their performances than are the observers. The main advantage of the modeling process, including the use of video, is that it gives participants the opportunity to perceive a situation that they would be likely to encounter in the real world and in which they may also be affected by the more subtle aspects of the performance. They may notice frowns, smiles, nods, shifts of stance, gestures, grunts, coughs, whispers, use of silences, pursing of lips, regulation of distance between model and partner, touching, and so on. These behaviors are open to interpretation and rely on such interpretation for their effect. This is precisely what is entailed in implicit communication. Implicit communication and the conveying of implicit demands is the dominant mode of communication among lovers, friends, members of the same family, school groups, and organizations in which physical proximity over time is established. In families, children spend time in trying to discern the moods and meanings of parents and older siblings by observing facial expressions. They are involved in a dependent relationship with their parents and siblings. They need to anticipate the reactions of their family members to their own behavior and to the behavior of others, friends, neighbors, schoolmates, playmates, and so forth.

Goldstein's (1999) Situational Perception Training emphasized alternative ways of understanding situations through group discussion and verbal analysis rather than through the use of role-plays. This approach was also more directed toward young people with severe behavioral problems, often in institutions. Facilitators selected situations from 182 different vignettes, and participants were asked to clarify the situation by discussing setting, purpose, and relationship. The following sample vignettes illustrate the range of situations depicted:

- The parole board has just held you another 6 months. You think you should be able to go home because you haven't broken any of the rules. What would you do?
- You are always doing the hardest work in the kitchen. None of the other workers is helping you out. What would you do?
- A resident who is a friend of yours tells you that he has just received a letter from his girlfriend and she has broken up with him. What would you do?
- A resident you know in another unit is upset because her parents, who promised to visit her for the past 3 weeks, have not shown up. What would you do?
- You have to go talk to a staff person, your teacher, to discuss an earlier incident in which you had been disrespectful and had cursed at her. What would you do?
- A staff member is angry with you because you have not followed her directions for cleaning up your office unit. What would you do?
- A resident has just been told that his parents are here for their visit, but he has been assigned to work in the kitchen. What would you do?
- You are walking down the street, and you notice a woman standing beside her car, which has a flat tire. What would you do?
- You've just been released home, and it's your first week in school. Some of your old friends have decided that they are going to skip the day and not go to school. They have asked you to come with them. What would you do?
- You have really made a lot of progress in your reading, and it's time for you to be released from the program. You must say good-bye to your reading teacher. What would you do?
- You have just received the results of your GED exam and have found out that you did not pass. What would you do?
- You and another resident have had a physical confrontation, and staff members tell you that you must sit down with him after lunch and work it out. What would you do?
- The cook who is serving the food is angry with you because he just heard you tell another resident how bad it tastes. What would you do?
- Your mother's boyfriend is drunk and getting a little nasty. It looks as though he's getting up to come over and hit you. What would you do?

The sessions described in the present book go beyond group discussion of situations to include modeling, role-playing, performance feedback, and generalization. Since the program has become quite different in content and structure from Goldstein's approach, the name of the program has been changed to Social Perception Training. The session focus is not only to teach specific skills, but also to develop different perspectives on how a situation can be interpreted and clarified and to further stimulate discussion on which skill or skills should be generated and performed. We use the term *emulation* to describe this process. Emulation can be generally defined as the attempt, by an observer, to equal or improve upon the performance of others. We use the term to describe the process whereby the observer's task is not merely to imitate the behavior of the model but also to understand the causes of and goals for performance and to improve upon the model's performance.

We thus extend the boundaries usually employed in modeling (specifically, exemplary modeling) to direct attention to the importance of applying social-perceptual skills when engaging in social interaction. We do not want observers to merely repeat these performances, but to improve upon the performances so that the actors achieve better results or management of the problem. This process involves the group's active observation and questioning of the models to enable them to generate plausible explanations as to the interaction's antecedents and to determine the models' goals. Participants are trained in attending to the situational resources and demands and the skills required for the best possible use of these resources.

## Session Content and Structure

The SPT program includes an introductory session plus a session devoted to each of the nine specific topic areas shown in Table 1. Each session could be divided into two parts depending on how deeply facilitators want to go into the topic. The program is therefore flexible and normally lasts between 10 and 20 sessions.

Each session has both an *external structure* and an *internal structure*, as shown in Table 2. The external structure includes components common to all sessions; the internal structure also follows a specific procedure, although the topic varies from session to session. We find it helpful to link the session topic with a specific image or icon. Full-page, reproducible versions of these images are included in Appendix A.

### External Structure

*Welcome and introduction*

Facilitators greet participants at the door and make some positive comments while checking that everyone is relatively calm. If someone is restless or agitated, the co-facilitator can take a walk and talk with that person and calm him or her down.

## Table 2: Social Perception Training Session Topics

| | |
|---|---|
| Session 1 | Introduction to Social Perception Training |
| Session 2 | Emotional Awareness |
| Session 3 | Open and Hidden Rules in Different Situations |
| Session 4 | Cultural Differences |
| Session 5 | Setting Events |
| Session 6 | Thoughts, Feelings, Body Signals, and Actions |
| Session 7 | Interpreting Others' Intentions |
| Session 8 | Cognitive Distortions |
| Session 9 | Timing (Right Time and Place) |
| Session 10 | Consequences (If-Then) |

**Table 3: Outline of Social Perception Training Session Structure**

**External Structure**

Welcome and introduction

Reminder of rules

Review of previous session and session homework

**Internal Structure**

1. Facilitators present the topic of the day

2. Facilitators present one situation

3. Participants analyze the situation

4. Participants suggest alternative ways of continuing the role-play

5. Participants choose one solution

6. Participants role-play the chosen solution

7. Facilitators and participants conduct feedback round

8. Facilitators and participants repeat Steps 4–7

9. Facilitators assign homework

**Continuation of External Structure**

Review of session

Wind-up

Closing of session

---

The session then continues with a regular group ritual. Here are some variants:

1. Participants all stand in a circle with their arms on each other's shoulders. They look around at each other and ask if anything has happened since last time that they would like to share with the group.

2. Participants all stand in a circle, extend their arms forward so that their hands lie on top of one another's, and, as they raise their arms in the air, shout "Yay, yay, SPT!" or some other cheer suggested by the participants.

3. We find that the following rehearsal has a calming effect before the session starts: Participants sit in their seats and raise their shoulders three times while breathing deeply. They place their left foot over their right foot and stretch both hands forward, the right hand placed over the left hand (like leading oneself by the hand). They twist their arms down and in toward their body while keeping them crossed against their chests. The participants start breathing deeply while listening to soothing music. A few seconds will do to begin with, but after a while they will be able to hold that position for a minute.

In SPT, we also have found it very helpful to begin the session by showing an optical illusion, like the one shown in Figure 3. In this way, there is an exciting start; the participants want to be the first to suggest the correct answer and hurry to session to avoid missing them. It is always exciting to see how a picture or a situation can change depending on what we actually perceive. Some aspects of a situation or a picture can make us perceive other aspects wrongly. Are these horizontal lines parallel, or do they slope?

Small exercises like this, along with small teasers or games, are very suitable in SPT training. You can find may examples of illusions like this on the Internet in the form of both still pictures and short videos. (YouTube has a wealth of possibilities.) These activities and the optical illusions can also be spread out and used to generate interest in other parts of the session.

### Reminder of rules

At the start of the program, and whenever the group is restless, one should remind them of the rules. Remember to ask the group rather than to tell them yourself. Suggested rules may be to participate actively, to come to the session on time, to keep what is said within the group, and to raise one's hand before speaking.

### Review of previous session and homework

Participants are asked what they did or practiced since the previous session in SPT. It is very important to have this repetition in each session because it connects the different program aspects and participants can thus recognize how these aspects are linked.

The facilitator collects the Social Perception Training Log, presented in Appendix C, which is the normal homework in SPT training (see Figure 4 for an example). It is important that those who have done their homework receive the praise they deserve. Do not read aloud a participant's homework or refer to it without permission. If someone has not done the homework, talk with him or her about it *after* the session and identify why the student did not complete the assignment. In some cases, it may be advantageous

## Figure 3: Sample Optical Illusion

# Figure 4: Sample Social Perception Training Log

Name _Eric Olson_      Session number _10_      Date _10/10_

1. What happened?

    *I was sleeping on the train, and suddenly a ticket collector woke me up and said loudly that I should take my feet from the opposite chair and remove my bag. I became angry and said that everybody did that.*

2. Did you identify any emotions in the other person?

    *She was quite angry.*

3. What emotions did you have yourself?

    *I was sleepy but became angry, too.*

4. What open or hidden rules could be present in the situation?

    *Probably that you should take off your shoes before you put your legs on the other chair and don't have your bag on the other seat if other people have to stand.*

5. Did you identify any cultural aspects that influenced the situation?

    *Maybe that you should offer a seat to elderly people—some were standing. Maybe that was why the ticket collector was angry.*

6. What possible setting events could have influenced the other's reaction?

    *The ticket collector might be irritated because she receives a lot of complaints from other passengers. Maybe she had a headache or slept badly.*

7. What possible setting events could have influenced your actions?

    *I was sleepy.*

8. Did you experience that your thoughts influenced your emotions, body feelings, or your actions?

    *Yes, I felt I became angry at once—even before I was thinking—and my action was that I said in an angry way that everybody puts their feet on the other chair. If I had given myself time to think, I might have put my feet down without commenting.*

9. What intentions do you think the other person had in the situation?

    *Probably to make it so everybody could sit on the train.*

10. What intentions did you have in the situation?

*To sleep, but I guess that her intention is more important.*

11. Did you identify any thoughts or statements that could be considered cognitive distortions during the situation?

*Yes, I said that everybody put their feet up, but that might not be a good excuse for doing it.*

12. Did you identify any example of bad timing in the situation?

*Yes, actually. The ticket collector could have asked me in a quiet way to take my feet down instead of doing it so loudly in front of with so many people. I was embarrassed because she shouted at me. It was her angry voice that made me angry—not that I had to put my feet down.*

13. Did you ask or do anything to clarify the situation to understand it better?

*No, I didn't. I might have asked her if I could have my feet on the chair before putting them up.*

14. What consequences did the interaction lead to?

*Hopefully, not that many negative ones. I managed to control myself and say that I was sorry. Maybe the train people will be better in explaining the rules.*

15. What can I say/say to myself when I succeed?

*I managed to apologize.*

16. What can I do better next time?

*Ask about the rules.*

17. What can the other person do better next time?

*Inform people of rules before getting mad.*

18. How did I handle the situation? (Circle one.)

| 1 | 2 | 3 | 4 | 5 | ⑥ | 7 | 8 | 9 | 10 |
|---|---|---|---|---|---|---|---|---|----|
| Badly | | | | | | | | Very well | |

to introduce reinforcement when all group members have completed a given number of assignments.

## Internal Structure

The internal structure is the main part of the session and includes the specific topic to be learned. Although the content varies from session to session, the internal structure follows steps described in detail in the following pages.

### 1. Facilitators present the topic of the day

The presentation of the topic is a very important part of the session. Each session has its own topic, representing 10 different perspectives for the understanding of a given social situation. The presentation of the topic of the day consists of the following:

- Identifying the concept or topic of the day. Define/present the topic. What do you think today's topic means? Facilitators write suggestions on the board and help to find a correct definition.

- One or two rehearsals. Each session should contain some exercises that demonstrate the topic of the day. Pictures or video clips presented using PowerPoint, followed by short rehearsals, are the usual mode of presenting the content of the session. In our experience, the use of PowerPoint presentations has proven to be of great help in communicating with participants. These presentations provide facilitators with an opportunity to prepare for each session using photos, videos, and optical illusions. It is also easy to enter participants' analyses and suggestions during the session and then print out the results. It is also important to vary the presentation form with small role-plays, rehearsals, and games in order to keep the interest of the participants.

- Identifying the need (i.e., why it is important to know about today's topic?).

- Possible situations in which today's topic is important. Facilitators provide examples of contexts or situations where and when it is important to take the specific topic into account. These examples can also be used as situations later in the session.

### 2. Facilitators present one situation

After the presentation of the content of the day, facilitators continue with a role-play of a social situation and subsequent reflections on the role-play, including suggestions on how to progress in the interaction. Facilitators choose a situation relevant for the session topic, adjusted according to the age and cognitive level of the participants. If appropriate, facilitators can refer to situations arising from the participants' homework. Appendix B provides suggested role-plays that deal with the different session topics.

Facilitators usually present the situation in the form of a brief role-playing but can also use other presentation forms, like video clips or storytelling. The presentation continues until the problem has been well presented. To avoid revealing the correct answers, "bubble talk," or expressing aloud what is normally thought to oneself, is not used during the presentation. In some cases, we analyze the situation from the perspective of one of the parties, but in other cases we prefer to analyze the situation from the perspectives of both or all parties. The option chosen is stated in advance.

### 3. Participants analyze the situation

The main facilitator helps the participants to clarify and analyze the situation and emphasizes the skill of observation in order to get the right understanding of the situation. The co-facilitator records the participants' suggestions on a whole-group display (e.g., PowerPoint, whiteboard, easel pad) and helps participants formulate appropriate comments. A skillful facilitator makes the participants more active than himself or herself. It is important to ask questions and ask "Is it OK to . . . ?" or "Could . . . be an example of . . . ?" to make them reflect and reformulate. Good facilitators also praise the participants continually for their suggestions. The Social Perception Training Reflection Form, provided in Appendix C, is helpful in guiding discussion of different aspects of the main role-play. It may be set up on a chalkboard or flip chart or presented as a PowerPoint display. Participants reflect on the different aspects of the role-play according to how far they have progressed in the training. Topics that are not relevant need not be discussed.

Facilitators allow participants to analyze the situation first and ask questions if there are important factors missing. It is important to try to choose questions relevant to the participants' cognitive ability. Some suggested questions are as follows:

- What is actually happening in the situation?
- Are there any other demands in the form of rules and norms that may be affecting the situation?
- Might the actors in the role-play represent different cultural norms?
- Can we identify the actors' emotional expressions?
- Could anything outside the situation have contributed to the actors' emotional state?
- Which *expressed* goals or intentions have the different actors shown in the situation?
- Are the actions of the different actors relevant to the situation?
- Are the different actors "tuned in" to each other?
- What are the roles, responsibilities, or expectations of the different actors?

### 4. Participants suggest alternative ways of continuing the role-play

When suggesting alternative ways of continuing the role-play, participants must argue why their solution is rewarding, correct, and fair for the different people in the play. It should also be possible to start the alternative continuation of the role-play *before* the end of the original one. We call this "finding the turning point(s)," which suggests that each response from each of the partners could be handled a different way and that all the new responses may prove to be a turning point that leads to a better conclusion. The important task for facilitators is to emphasize that there are *always* alternative responses to use in any and all situations. However, some responses may have a more negative influence on partners than others. It is very important to identify the action or actions at the moment the conflict escalates (this is the concept of "triggers" in Prepare's Anger Control Training) and be able to suggest an alternative response.

## 5. Participants choose one solution

The solution or solutions matching the criteria in Item 4 are chosen to continue the role-play. At this point, it could be an advantage to divide the group into two, if it is larger than five members. Each subgroup chooses the best solution and role-plays it. When choosing participants for particular roles, it can be a good idea to put them in roles that they do not identify with. This can enhance their ability to consider an episode from different viewpoints.

## 6. Participants plan and role-play the chosen solution

The next step is to role-play the chosen solution. Two or three participants prepare the continuation of the role-play with the co-facilitator, while the main facilitator gives the other participants evaluation tasks such as these:

- Did the actors consider the others' intention and goal for the interaction?
- Did the actors follow the explicit and implicit situational rules appropriately?
- Did they respect each other's culture?

Questions like these may lead to simple yes and no answers from participants, so it is best to try to help them make more specific observations (e.g., one particular goal that an actor got out of the interaction or which nonverbal cue from actor B was noticed by actor A). During the role-play, the facilitators can choose whether to use bubble talk or not. The advantage of doing so is that the participants are guided in reasoning through the situation. However, bubble talk can take some of the points away from the observers.

## 7. Facilitators and participants conduct feedback round

After the role-play, the observers and the actors evaluate their performance. The observers give their comments first, followed by the facilitators and the actors. The actors are asked to recall whether they considered any situational factors during the role-play and which actions they performed that they experienced as being positive and contributing to a successful conclusion. It may be advantageous to link the facilitators' comments to personal qualities (you weren't scared, you showed respect, you behaved like a good friend). This can increase participants' awareness of the relationship between specific behavior and desirable personal qualities.

## 8. Facilitators and participants repeat Steps 4–7

If time allows, participants can role-play other difficult situations that they have experienced themselves or facilitators can propose specific new role-plays for them. Normally, time does not allow a full review of all the steps, but it is easy to conduct shorter reviews. One example could involve having facilitators demonstrate poor ways to make contact with older friends. Participants can stop behavior they believe is wrong by pointing an imaginary remote control (moynahan, 2003) at one of the actors and saying "stop" and then telling the actor what went wrong with the role-playing. To allow more participants to take part in the role-playing, you can let any participant who makes a good suggestion as to what to do next change places with the person currently playing the role. This way of conducting dilemma discussions is very motivating.

## 9. Facilitators assign homework

As noted previously, the regular homework is to fill out the Social Perception Training Log (provided in Appendix C). This form can also be used as an assessment tool to reflect how the participants interpret a social situation in a more and more complex way. Participants should be instructed to fill out the Social Perception Training Log up to the point of training. For example, after Session 2, participants fill out items 1 through 3. As sessions progress they fill out more and more of the form according to the content of each session.

## Continuation of External Structure

### Review of the session

After completing the day's topic, the facilitator asks what was done during the session, what the most important points were, and how the topic learned can be applied. (It is also important to summarize content when moving from one theme to another and, as suggested in the sessions themselves, to review the content of the previous session at the beginning of each new one.)

### Wind-up

Winding up with a group ritual is a good way of rounding off the session. A popular feature in many groups is the "friendship round." The purpose is to develop positive feelings in the group and to thank one another for good teamwork. This can be done in several ways:

- Each participant says something positive about everyone else in the group.
- Each participant says something positive to the group.
- Each participant says something positive about the person sitting on the left—and so it goes around the circle.
- Each participant says something he or she has done well and something he or she could have done differently. The facilitator always gives an example first.

We have had very good experience with these activities. Participants come to greatly appreciate hearing compliments about themselves and become better at observing positive things about others. They also forge better relationships with one another through this type of activity.

### Topic of the next session

It is important at this point to give participants a short briefing on the topic for the next session.

### Closing of session

Toward the end of the session, certificates recognizing good effort or program completion might be handed out. This recognition can be important, but it must not be exaggerated or the reinforcement loses its value. Finally, the sessions are concluded with a cheer or similar ritual.

## Role-Play Variation

In smaller groups from 6 to 10 participants, facilitators can make the session even more interactive by dividing the group into two and let each group perform a situation. The following procedure is suggested for encouraging a combination of group discussion and role-play as an alternative to be used in some of the sessions.

1. Planning the role-play: The group is divided into two equal smaller groups, and both groups are given or instructed to select a challenging situation. Group A receives coaching from the main facilitator on how to perform the role-play and performs until the critical moment (the turning point).

2. Analyzing the role-play: Under guidance of the co-facilitator, members of Group B are asked to discuss what they have seen. Through this process, efforts are made to ensure that the sequence is perceived accurately according to Bellack et al.'s (2004) categories (listening, clarification, relevance, timing, and identification of emotions). Basically, this means that the role-play is understood correctly and that participants generate possible motives, emotional states, goals, and demands for the different actors. Questions about timing, relevance, and cultural aspects may also be asked. In the early stages of the training, Group B can ask the models in Group A for information.

3. Suggesting possible solutions to the problem: Participants in Group B are then required to suggest possible solutions to the problem. The most pragmatic solution (or the most rewarding, moral, fair, etc.) must then be chosen, and Group B is asked to role-play the resolution as a model for improvement.

4. Evaluation by Group A: Members of Group A are given the task of evaluating Group B's solutions and their explanations for their choice. Group judgment is then given on the basis of the following criteria: (a) practicality of the solution, (b) novelty of the solution, and (c) perceived justice of the solution.

5. Group B self-evaluation: Each role-player evaluates the resolution from his or her perspective on the basis of these questions: (a) Did I achieve a good result for myself and the group? and (b) Did I contribute to any problems for the group?

6. Following role-play: Group B performs their role-play, and the process continues according to Steps 2 through 5.

This basic format may be used sequentially to challenge triads, pairs, and individual participants. The larger group may challenge randomly constructed triads to avoid formation of alliances of two against one (exclusion), which may hinder the generation of alternative perceptions or interpretations or reduce the number or quality of pragmatic solutions.

When the larger group challenges randomly constructed pairs of participants, they are effectively challenging the pair's ability to cooperate. In this case, we usually reduce the time allowed for the pair to suggest alternative perceptions and select the most pragmatic way of dealing with the situation. In challenging individuals, the group presents episodes where the actions of one person are of central importance. Role-plays highlight the importance of being able to take into account the differing perspectives held by the various actors. This challenges the individual participant's ability to generate perceptual alternatives, ascertain the motives and goals of the actors, and provide pragmatic solutions that maintain the rights and dignity of those concerned.

## Program Implementation Concerns

SPT can be used with both children and adolescents, in combination with other Pre-pare courses or as a program of its own. The ideal age for starting the SPT program seems to be between 10 and 14, but it is also possible to adapt examples and rehearsals to younger and older participants. The program can be run either as an independent program for a whole class or for a smaller group of approximately eight participants. It is less expensive to implement the program in a whole class, but the possibility for involvement of each student is greater in a smaller group.

We recommend an additional five sessions with the participants and their families, if at all possible. In the first of these sessions, the program is presented to the parents only. The remaining sessions focus specifically on unwritten rules and norms, cultural differences (age differences), setting events, and intentions. We have also had good experience with SPT as a supplemental program after students have received ART.

As described by Dean Fixen and colleagues in *Implementation Research: A Synthesis of the Literature* (Fixsen, Naoom, Blase, Friedman, & Wallace, 2005), proper implementation of a program is as important as the quality of the program itself. In several meta-analyses, lack of implementation quality has correlated with lack of program effect (Payne, Gottfredson, & Gottfredson, 2006; Wilson & Lipsey, 2007). Key factors for proper implementation of a program are the quality of the program leader, which also includes training standards and pedagogical procedures; support for the program leader, including integration of the program in the whole organization; and continued plans for conducting the program, including practical issues like location as well as supervision and evaluation.

A single program leader should be appointed to be responsible for the SPT activities in the organization. Support for the program leader is the most important factor for success in implementing a program for training social competence (Olsen & Gundersen, 2012). After determining the need for the program, the leader decides both how many and who should be trained to deliver it. It is an advantage if the teachers who are going to offer the program are motivated to do so, but it may also be helpful to involve some of the more skeptical teachers. After training, teachers who are initially negative become positive. In Norway, the certification of SPT group facilitators includes three days of training in conducting the different sessions. Facilitator quality encompasses both pedagogical skills and knowledge of the program.

After training the group facilitators, the program leader grants money to prepare the program, organizes the schedule to allow time for the SPT program, and decides whether the program should be carried out for the whole class or smaller groups. If the group facilitator is not the regular teacher of the class, it is a big advantage if the teacher also can attend the sessions. Normally, issues discussed during the session will come up in other school subjects, and it strengthens the program for teachers to refer to what students have learned or will learn in SPT.

Included in the program leader's role is giving information about the program to other staff members and parents, organizing the schedule for the SPT activities in the school, and evaluating the program. The program leader also normally designs the PowerPoint presentations for the different sessions, using age-relevant pictures, rehearsals, and video clips. He or she also suggests when the program should start and end, introduces evaluation forms, finds a suitable room, obtains necessary equipment, and provides posters of group rules and other information for the different sessions. To prevent the program from "drifting," it is also very important to provide or secure adequate supervision and to have options available if some of the group facilitators become ill or leave the job.

Program fidelity forms, included in Appendix D, are designed to ensure that facilitators accurately follow the recommended steps in program delivery. The Social Perception Training Facilitator's Evaluation Form should be completed after each session. In order to secure that all the elements are included in a session and thus secure program fidelity, it is also very useful to use the checklist when planning the session. This form, and an observer's checklist, are included in the appendix. Further adherence to implementation integrity can be promoted by videotaping the sessions to be reviewed in peer supervision by a coach or master trainer.

## Preliminary Program Evaluation

The SPT program is currently being evaluated in Norway. In one study (Strømgren, Gundersen, & Svartdal, 2013), participants (52 children from grades 4 and 6) were assigned to SPT or comparison groups based on a matched randomization procedure from teachers' pretest scores. The SPT group received an intervention consisting of 10 to 20 sessions of 45 minutes each, based on the Norwegian version of the program (Gundersen & Valjord, 2011). The comparison group received their regular scheduled classroom teaching.

The Social Skills Rating System (SSRS; Gresham & Elliott, 1990) was used to measure changes in social skills and problem behaviors before and after the SPT delivery. Data were obtained from the teachers and parents. Included was an assessment of usefulness of the program from those students who received the SPT intervention, in the form of 12 questions that could be answered on a Likert scale ranging from 1 (useful to a small degree) to 4 (useful to a large degree).

Preliminary results from the teachers and parents joint scores are encouraging. Both group scores showed a statistically significant overall improvement in social skill scores, with a greater improvement for the SPT group than for the comparison group. The students judged the program and its contents as useful, with 75 to 100 percent rating the program useful to a "medium" (3) "large" (4) degree. At a post-training evaluation, parents also judged the program to be a useful program for their children.

Preliminary results appear encouraging because the training was delivered as a stand-alone intervention and not in concert with another program, such as Aggression Replacement Training (ART; Glick & Gibbs, 2011; Goldstein, Glick, & Gibbs, 1998). In the ART program, the three different interventions work toward the same goal at the same time but emphasize different dimensions of social competence in a "cross-fertilization" manner (in other words, the different programs support one another). The SPT intervention varied in length, with some participants receiving only 10 sessions. With this perspective in mind, future delivery of SPTcould include fewer sessions and might also benefit from combination with other programs. Goldstein's (1999) Prepare Curriculum is a natural source for other program components to deliver in connection with SPT.

# PART 2

## Social Perception Training Sessions

# SESSION 1
# Introduction to Social Perception Training

## AIM OF THE SESSION

To provide an overview of the program and motivate participants to participate actively

## PROCEDURE

1.  Give an introduction to perception by showing an optical illusion in a drawing or video clip. This clearly illustrates to young people that things are not always what they seem. Explain that an optical illusion occurs when we perceive an image to be different from what it really is. The information sent from our eyes to our brain challenges our perception of reality. Explain that *perception* means interpreting or giving a meaning to something one experiences.

2.  Role-play with your co-facilitator or show a video clip involving an ambiguous situation. For example, a girl is waiting for her boyfriend. A boy comes over and asks the way to the movie theater. The girl's boyfriend sees them talking together and walks away. How might the boyfriend interpret this—first, when he hasn't heard what they said, and second, when he has heard it? Reflect upon what happened and how the boyfriend's thoughts about the other boy's intention may influence how the boyfriend reacts. Remember to use suitable language for the group.

3.  Point out that in social situations we receive many signals, both verbal and nonverbal. At the same time, the situation we are in is likely to have its own rules. Explain that the aim of the program is to raise participants' understanding of ways to interpret social situations, thus enabling them to make better choices in subsequent interactions. Reality is not always what we believe it to be: A Mercedes rushes past us on the motorway. Is the driver showing off? Is he a snob? Maybe he's going to the hospital. Sometimes we interpret an event in the light of the characteristics we apply to another person (e.g., that he's a snob, from another culture, mean, annoying). On other occasions, we may consider factors in the situation itself: He's driving to the hospital, he needs money, and so forth. Such matters can determine not only how we interpret the situation but also the subsequent interaction.

4.  Give participants one minute to identify all the green items in the classroom. After they identifying the green objects, ask them to identify objects of another color.

By doing this, we illustrate that we normally perceive what we are looking for. Reflect on another example, like one person who spends time identifying hairstyles among spectators while watching a soccer match while others know and can talk about both the players who have scored and the ones who have given assists to those who scored.

5.  Give each participant a copy of the Social Perception Training Session Outline. Briefly describe the content of each session, preferably with the aid of illustrations or video clips. Explain that the course will include training in both receiving and processing the information we obtain from social settings and also help us to choose suitable responses.

6.  To get participants to play an active role in the session, encourage them to think about what Social Perception Training is and why it is useful: It helps you to achieve your goals, not make a fool of yourself, not hurt other people's feelings, not get angry or make others angry, not risk being frozen out, and so on.

    *The use of humor is very helpful in sensitizing what can go wrong when people do not use the appropriate skills when they fall victim to illusions and misconstrue what is happening. TV sitcoms are a good source of examples.*

7.  Draw up group rules together with the participants. The group should generate its own ideas, but some common helpful rules are as follows:

    -   Come to the session on time.
    -   Keep what is said within the group.
    -   Be respectful.
    -   Raise your hand before speaking.

# Social Perception Training Session Outline

| | |
|---|---|
| | ***Session 1: Introduction to Social Perception Training***<br><br>To *perceive* means to interpret or give meaning to what we observe. In the sessions, we will take a close look at some common social situations in which it is easy to be misunderstood or to misunderstand others. These misunderstandings may lead to conflict, loss of friendships, and other difficult situations. The object of the program is to learn social rules and norms to better handle these difficult social situations. |
| | ***Session 2: Emotional Awareness***<br><br>The ability to communicate our own feelings and also take into consideration other people's worries and emotions is the key to social success. If we can't interpret others' feelings and experience from others' perspectives, we can easily interpret social signals incorrectly and be confused about how we should react in an acceptable way. |
| | ***Session 3: Open and Hidden Rules in Different Situations***<br><br>Open rules are explicitly expressed and fairly easy to learn. Hidden rules are implicitly expressed rules that just occur within a culture or situation and that we need to master to avoid behaving in a socially unacceptable way. |
| | ***Session 4: Cultural Differences***<br><br>Cultural differences are differences in the ways groups do things. For example, different nations and ethnic cultures may have different hidden and open rules. Different subcultures may have different rules within larger nations or groups—for example, there may be different expectations for males and females or young people and adults. |
| | ***Session 5: Setting Events***<br><br>Often we bring experiences, thoughts, emotions, or physiological status (like pain or tiredness) from one situation to another. These setting events are important because they influence the way we think and act, even if they are not directly connected to the situation we are in. |

| | |
|---|---|
| | **Session 6: Thoughts, Feelings, Body Signals, and Actions** <br><br> How we think about or interpret a situation can affect our feelings, body signals, and actions. Sometimes our feelings and body signals come first, and we might interpret a situation on the basis of how we feel and not on what we think. Changes in any one of these factors will have an impact on the others. |
| | **Session 7: Interpreting Others' Intentions** <br><br> An intention is what you or another wishes to achieve in a certain situation. For example, you might want to be kind or get something. It is important to be able to interpret others' intentions because this interpretation will influence how we react and respond. |
| | **Session 8: Cognitive Distortions** <br><br> Cognitive distortions, sometimes called thinking errors, are things we tell ourselves to justify actions we actually know are not right. This way of justifying our actions is called *self-centered*. There are three categories within of self-centeredness: *blaming others, minimizing,* and *assuming the worst.* Understanding our thinking errors helps us to take responsibility for our actions. |
| | **Session 9: Timing (Right Time and Place)** <br><br> Timing means the right time and place for an action. To get along with others, it is important to be able to distinguish between situations where a specific action might be proper and where it might be considered wrong. It is also very important to know *when* to act and *when* to wait. Sometimes it is important to interrupt a conversation, to change the subject of the conversation, and so on. Knowing when to do this is an important skill. |
| | **Session 10: Consequences (If-Then)** <br><br> Consequences are what happen after an action, right away or after some time has gone by. Consequences might be good or bad. Evaluating consequences helps us to predict what will happen and make better choices in the future. |

# SESSION 2
# Emotional Awareness

## AIM OF THE SESSION

To improve participants' ability to identify, differentiate, and express basic feelings and to increase their capacity to react to other people's feelings in a positive way

## THEORETICAL BASIS

The importance of emotional awareness, including identifying and expressing emotions, is one of the key factors in social competence (Hallberstadt, Denham, & Dunsmore, 2001). Children with difficulties interpreting other people's emotional status seem to be more disliked and are also in danger of being rejected by their peers (Fabes et al., 1999). The skill of dealing with emotions involves the abilities to understand our own emotions, to identify others' emotions, and to respond properly when others are showing emotions (Denham et al., 2003). The internal dimension of identifying emotions includes understanding what the various emotions signal, deciding which emotions are associated with different situations, and determining which emotions have their origin in internal and external events (Stifter, 2002). Understanding another person's emotional state in a given social situation requires the ability to identify both verbal and nonverbal communication (e.g., facial expressions, voice tone and pace, gestures, and body position). Body language may also involve communication that is quite clear, but at the same time hidden—for example, looking at your watch or yawning when you are tired and want someone to go. We seem to have six major emotional expressions: anger, happiness, surprise, fear, disgust, and sadness (see Buck, 1984). Even though various cultures display emotions differently, considerable evidence exists that these six emotions, and possibly more, appear to be cross-cultural (Ekman, Friesen, & Ellsworth, 1982).

The more we practice understanding our own and others' feelings, the more automatic our ability to do so becomes. Such component skills need to be fluent. Behavioral fluency is described as a fluid combination of accuracy plus speed (Binder, 1996). This description fits in well with what is needed in real-life social situations: One must identify the other person's emotion correctly, and the correct identification needs to be made quickly. Goldstein (1999) has commented upon a similar prerequisite that may help transfer training—namely, the concept of "overlearning" linked to the slogan "Perfect training of perfect makes perfect." Lack of behavioral fluency is also described as one of three major deficits (together with acquisition deficits and performance deficits) when social skills or social competence are inadequate (Elliott & Gresham, 1991). Special training in the identification of emotions in others may thus be well advised.

# PROCEDURE

*Conduct a friendship round or other opening ritual and share an optical illusion. Remind participants of rules and review the previous session.*

## Step 1

1. Identify the concept or topic of the day: Define and discuss identifying emotions. Show the six basic emotions by using pictures, video clips or demonstrations. Ask the group what they think emotional awareness means and discuss. Write the group's suggestions on a whole-group display and assist participants in getting the concept right. If necessary, paraphrase the following:

   > Emotional awareness is the ability to communicate our own feelings and also take into consideration other people's worries and emotions. It is the key to social success. If we can't interpret others' feelings and experience from the others' perspective, we can easily interpret social signals incorrectly and be confused about how we should react in an acceptable way.

2. Ask participants to describe situations when they get the different feelings. For example:

   I become angry when . . .

   I become sad when . . .

   I feel joyful when . . .

   *It is useful to present pictures that illustrate different emotions.*

3. Choose from among the following or make up your own exercises according to the capabilities of participants. Start by identifying emotions and carefully expand: identifying feelings, understanding the emotions, and acting according to the emotion and situation. Emphasize facial expressions, tone of voice, and other body language.

### Exercise 1

The group is divided into two (if there are at least eight participants). Each group presents four different variations on a sentence like "I am going to Grandpa and Grandma's house." The sentence is to be expressed with different emotional nuances (e.g., very sad, disappointed, surprised, very happy). Other suitable sentences might be "Today we're having sausages for dinner" or "Pete's invited me to a movie."

### Exercise 2

Write down five feelings (sad, excited, happy, angry, and scared) on pieces of paper and put them into a hat. The group members sit on their chairs in a circle. One of the group members draws a feeling out of the hat while the others sit on chairs in a circle. His or her chair is taken away. If the feeling is happy, he or she tries to mime the feeling and the others guess which feeling it is. When the feeling is guessed, the person that mimed says, "I will be happy if I _____ (e.g., get a compliment)."

The participants who are happy about the same thing change chairs. The one who drew the feeling hurries to sit down on one of the chairs while the others change so there will be someone who doesn't find a chair. The person without a chair then draws a feeling out of the hat.

### Exercise 3

Write down the six basic emotions on pieces of paper (sadness, happiness, anger, fear, disgust, and surprise). Someone draws a slip of paper and role-plays the emotion (using facial expressions and body language). The others sit in a semicircle and try to identify the emotion. The one who identifies the emotion first comes and draws another piece of paper and role-plays the emotion. Before starting, decide how long to do this exercise (from 2–5 minutes). If you use this exercise several times, you can see if it is possible to increase the number of identified emotions.

### Exercise 4

Hand out "remote controls" made of cardboard to the participants. View a video clip. If the participants identify an emotion, they press a button, say "Stop," and stop the action with the remote control. The participant who stops the action says which emotion he or she identified and how he or she identified it. The video is then started again and stopped when the next person identifies an emotion. This continues until the end of the movie clip. (Suggested video clip: *Shrek 2,* where Donkey teases Shrek.)

4. Identify the need: Write reasons it may be important to recognize one's own and others' emotions.

5. Identify and write down possible situations where the concept of understanding emotions is important. Note the names of students who make these suggestions.

### Exercise 5

A simple, quick, and fun way of training this component skill is to base the training upon precision teaching principles (Binder, 1996) and arrange training "spurts" within the group. One participant stands in the middle of a circle composed of the other participants and facilitators (see Figure 5). Facilitators and participants in the circle display an emotion—to start with, just facial expressions. The participant in the middle describes the emotions displayed by the group, beginning at 12 o'clock and turning clockwise until he or she has completed the circle, by which time the person at 12 o'clock and the rest of the circle have changed their emotional expressions. Typical spurt timing is 15, 20, 30, or 60 seconds, and the goal for the participant in the middle is to correctly identify as many emotions as possible within this time frame. A total of one or two minutes a day per participant should be enough to ensure fluent description within the time frame of the Social Perception Training program.

To ensure success in the early training spurt, the people in the circle could display only two or three emotions for the participant in the middle to identify (e.g., happy, sad, and angry). By having each basic emotion demonstrated by three or more participants, the one in the middle may be alerted to the similarities and unique differences all people have in expressing similar emotions. When identification is

## Figure 5: Training to Identify Emotions Based on Facial Expression

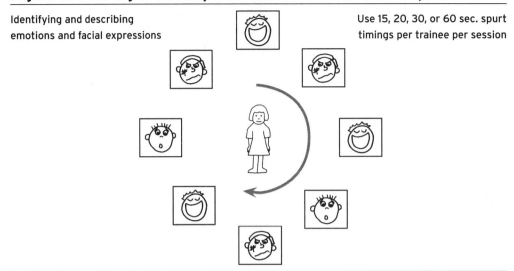

Identifying and describing emotions and facial expressions

Use 15, 20, 30, or 60 sec. spurt timings per trainee per session

fluent (i.e., a high enough rate of correct identifications combined with just a few or no errors), a new emotion may be introduced for those in the circle to display. The number of possible emotions to display may thus be expanded as one sees fit, and facial expressions in combination with body stance may also be added. The participants and facilitators in the circle decide what constitutes "correct identification," and participants acknowledge the interpretation of the expression made by the person in the middle. Facilitators may try out identifying emotions themselves to find a realistic rate to aim for.

### Steps 2-9

*After the presentation of the topic of the day, the session follows the usual structure (see pages 30–33 for procedure details).*

- **STEP 2:** Facilitators present one situation. (See suggested role-plays, Appendix B.)
- **STEP 3:** Participants analyze the situation. (Display the Social Perception Training Reflection Form, Appendix C.)
- **STEP 4:** Participants suggest alternative ways of continuing the role-play.
- **STEP 5:** Participants choose one solution.
- **STEP 6:** Participants role-play the chosen solution.
- **STEP 7:** Facilitators and participants conduct feedback round.
- **STEP 8:** Facilitators and participants repeat Steps 4–7 as time allows.
- **STEP 9:** Facilitators provide homework assignment.

*Hand out copies of the Social Perception Training Log (Appendix C) and answer any questions. Briefly review the session, conduct a friendship round or other group ritual, describe the topic for the next session, and recognize participants for their efforts.*

# SESSION 3
# Open and Hidden Rules in Different Situations

## AIM OF THE SESSION

To identify hidden and implicit rules for social interaction, both in general and in various specific settings

## THEORETICAL BASIS

Our behavior is governed by laws, rules, expectations, and norms. Some of these are common knowledge; others are more specifically connected to a particular culture or setting. By *open* or *overt rules and norms* we mean explicit rules that are clear, descriptive, and well-known (e.g., the laws of a nation, group rules on a poster, a no-smoking sign, various regulations). By *hidden* or *covert rules and norms*, however, we mean implicit rules that govern behavior expected within the culture or subculture. These rules and norms govern behavioral exchanges that have occurred countless times among all members of the culture over centuries. These hidden rules may vary or change from epoch to epoch, from situation to situation, and from culture to culture. Importantly, rules may vary from generation to generation, and it is therefore important to consider the value of Social Perception Training in courses designed to be conducted with children, young people, parents, and other adults.

Do the following rules hold true, and if so, where?

- Only the bride can wear a white dress at a wedding.
- Take off your hat when you enter a house.
- Give up your seat to an elderly person on the bus.
- Pay for the girl if you're out on a date.
- At a urinal, don't stand right next to another person.
- Say hello to everybody if you arrive at a party where there are ten guests.

Covert rules are conveyed via various verbal and (mostly) nonverbal signals, such as hints, gazing at another person or avoiding eye contact, looking at one's watch, facial expressions (e.g., frowns, smiles, looks of resignation), and various other gestures and body language, including maintaining distance or moving closer to another person.

In Social Perception Training, implicit rules are made explicit. This is an excellent way to introduce the young participants to the norms valid in different settings. What are the norms in a cinema, at a funeral, at school, in your club, in your group of friends? A norm denotes a set of expectations with regard to how one ought to behave. In some cases, one also takes on a role (e.g., parent-child, teacher-pupil, shop assistant-customer), where each roles will have different expectations and norms. Role expectations help us to regulate situations but may also lead to confusion if the role sets are perceived differently. Breaking laws and explicit rules usually has some kind of punishment as a consequence. Such consequences also apply to covert rules and norms, but in this case exclusion from the social group will often be the consequence. It is thought provoking that the punishments connected to both explicit laws and rules and implicit norms are the same regardless of whether the individual knew them or not.

An understanding of the concept of an "intimate zone" is useful to convey in this session. Where do we draw the lines between our intimate zone, friend zone, group zone, and public zone? What can we talk about and where? When do we cross the privacy line? The concept of *zone distances* (Hall, 1966) is helpful in this regard:

Intimate zone: Touching to 18 inches (46 cm)

Personal zone: 18 inches to 4 feet (46 cm–1.2 m)

Social zone: 4 to 8 feet (1.2 m–3.6 m)

Public zone: More than 8 feet (2.4 m) away

Zone distances are moderated by four distinct factors, which all affect one another: physical proximity, the direction one is facing (facing toward or away from the other person or standing side by side) regulating eye contact, and conversing about personal matters. One can stand very close to another person on a bus but compensate for the violation of the other person's intimate zone by looking away and standing side by side. Talking about personal matters in a car can often be a positive experience because there is no eye contact and the speakers do not facing each other. Facilitators should try to demonstrate that such ways of adapting to situations are examples of covert rules.

Another useful concept to introduce is *matching* (i.e., how we conform to another person's signals). We usually adapt intuitively to our interaction partner by mimicking body position, tone of voice, and tempo. If there is too much of a mismatch, it will appear that we are not in contact with our partner.

However, give priority to what you consider important for this session. Base your priorities on the participants' particular problems and find out their exact needs.

## PROCEDURE

*Welcome the group and, if desired, conduct an opening ritual and share an optical illusion. Remind participants of rules, review the previous session, and discuss the previous session's homework.*

### Step 1

1. Identify the concept or topic of the day: Define and discuss the idea of covert/ hidden and overt/open rules. Ask participants what they think these concepts mean and write suggestions on a whole-group display. If necessary, paraphrase:

Open rules are explicitly expressed and fairly easy to learn. Hidden rules are implicitly expressed rules that just occur within a culture or specific situation and that we need to master to avoid behaving in a socially unacceptable way.

2. Ask participants to identify some covert rules in different settings (e.g., on a bus, at a funeral, in a movie theater).

3. Conduct one or two exercises: Choose from among the following or make up your own exercises according to the capabilities of participants.

### Exercise 1

Brainstorm about the various open and hidden rules in different situations. Get the participants to identify overt and covert rules in different situations. It is best to choose situations typical of young people, such as the following:

- Driving a car
- Talking on one's mobile phone (about what and where)
- At a movie theater
- Having dinner at a friend's house with his or her parents
- At a security check at the airport

With a boyfriend/girlfriend (When are you dating someone? When can you go out with the ex of your friend? How many dances can you dance with others when you have a boyfriend/girlfriend? Can you give someone else a hug when your boyfriend/girlfriend is looking?)

### Exercise 2

What often lies behind a conflict is a disagreement about the various possible implicit norms in the situation. Read the following story and discuss whether this conflict situation is about hidden rules.

> Sue is watching television. Ken comes by and starts watching the same program as Sue. After a while, they go and eat. When they've finished eating, they go back to the TV. Ken picks up the remote and switches channels. Sue gets annoyed and says she was watching TV first, so she should decide what they're going to watch.

### Exercise 3

The basis of this exercise is the concepts of an intimate zone, friend zone, group zone, and public zone—specifically, how near to sit and what to talk about. A second part of this exercise could be to divide the participants into two groups and have them stand opposite one another in twos. Tell them to close their eyes and step quietly toward each other to try to get a feeling for where the intimate zone begins. Vary the exercise by approaching each other shoulder to shoulder and facing away from each other. Combine with intense eye contact. Discuss what feels comfortable within the different zones and how level of comfort is moderated by eye contact and standing sideways.

## Exercise 4

This scenario has several hidden rules. Read it carefully and help participants identify these rules. Remember, the rules are not stated, but they are expected!

> Miranda is a young businesswoman with a job in a big office building in a local city. She walks into the building and pushes the button for the elevator. When other people see her get on, they immediately walk out of the elevator. A person new to the building walks toward the elevator. Miranda raises her eyebrows and gives him a piercing look. He suddenly stops and backs away and does not get on the elevator. Miranda smiles a knowing smile and hits the button to go up to the twenty-third floor. Her staff on this floor has heard from the receptionist that she is on her way up. Suddenly, they move to put on their black jackets and their fancy black Prada shoes. They move everything off their desks and leave a single rose in a vase. Miranda sweeps off the elevator and walks briskly by each desk. She stops at the new girl's desk and looks sternly down at the top of the desk. The office girl looks at her desk and sees that she has left a picture of her parents there. Miranda gives a piercing look and waits. The girl hurriedly removes the picture. Miranda smiles a smile of satisfaction and goes into her office and shuts the door.

4. Identify the need. Ask participants why they think it is important to know about open and hidden rules. Record their responses. For example:

   - If someone comes too close to you, you might step away.
   - If you have been to a party, you might send a message to the host to say thanks.

5. Identify possible situations where the concept is important. Write down situations in which it is important to understand open and hidden rules. Also note the names of students who make suggestions.

## Steps 2–9

*After the presentation of the topic of the day, the session follows the usual structure (see pages 30–33 for procedure details).*

- **STEP 2:** Facilitators present one situation. (See suggested role-plays, Appendix B.)
- **STEP 3:** Participants analyze the situation. (Display the Social Perception Training Reflection Form, Appendix C.)
- **STEP 4:** Participants suggest alternative ways of continuing the role-play.
- **STEP 5:** Participants choose one solution.
- **STEP 6:** Participants role-play the chosen solution.
- **STEP 7:** Facilitators and participants conduct feedback round as time allows.
- **STEP 8:** Facilitators and participants repeat Steps 4–7.
- **STEP 9:** Facilitators assign homework.

*Hand out copies of the Social Perception Training Log as homework and answer any questions. Briefly review the session, conduct a friendship round or other group ritual, describe the topic for the next session, and recognize participants for their efforts.*

# SESSION 4
# Cultural Differences

## AIM OF THE SESSION

To increase participants' awareness of cultural differences, broadly defined, and to challenge sterotyping and overgeneralization of such differences.

## THEORETICAL BACKGROUND

This session is closely connected to the previous one because cultural differences are usually expressed in terms of implicit norms and rules, not explicitly formulated laws. For young immigrants, it is especially important to know the codes of the new country. What is the meaning of a smile to a stranger? In some cultures, a smile from a man entering a café to another man would be interpreted as a greeting, whereas in others, it would be seen as an invitation from a homosexual or as just plain stupid or offensive. A smile from a woman to a man could be seen as mere politeness or as a sexual invitation, depending entirely on the culture. It is important that the group discuss the typical codes in the country and culture where the training is taking place. The conduct of many young people is based on a youth culture that sometimes glorifies risky behavior. Yet such behavior in other settings like the workplace, school, or adult life may be considered unsuitable or offensive, leading to exclusion. Codes of this kind should also be discussed in the group. Systematic differences between cultures and subcultures also seem to exist regarding attitudes toward aggression, when it is appropriate to smile, whether men may cry, and so forth. (Ekman et al., 1982). There is a well-documented difference in how aggression is manifested in the southern versus northern United States (Nisbett & Cohen, 1996). In the south, a common way of confronting provocation is to retaliate, so as not to lose face ("culture of honor"), while in the northern states, the reaction is usually more rational and nonaggressive. In Europe, such culturally determined differences in aggression patterns are becoming ever more prominent in the context of increased immigration and greater social and geographical mobility. The world is becoming increasingly urbanized, with greater numbers of the world population living in larger cities. This population mix increases the demand for adequate socialization and sensitization toward norms and rules for interaction.

It may be difficult to differentiate between the previous session, on open and hidden rules, and this one because hidden rules are also involved in this session. In this session on cultural differences we emphasize "differences" in norms and rules depending on which culture you belong to as a person, while in Session 3 we focused on differences depending on situation or setting. For example, a family will create their own open and hidden rules that differ from other families and are defined as a culture.

When discussing cultural differences it is crucially important that the facilitators also challenge stereotyping and overgeneralizing. For example, it is a frequent mistake to think that elderly people or people from different ethnic cultures act more in opposition to, or divergent from, mainstream culture than is actually the case. In the session, it is therefore important both to discuss what may be the cultural origins of supposed differences and at the same time to reflect on the veracity or truthfulness in ascribing different social practices to people merely because of age or ethnicity.

# PROCEDURE

*Welcome the group and, if desired, conduct an opening ritual and share an optical illusion. Remind participants of rules, review the previous session, and discuss the previous session's homework.*

## Step 1

1. Identify the concept or topic of the day: Define and discuss the concept of cultural differences. Ask the group what they think the concept means. Write the group's suggestions on a whole-group display and help participants get the concept right. If necessary, paraphrase the following ideas. If possible, show pictures that express differences depending on culture. (This makes it easier to maintain the structure.)

   - Male versus female culture: Sometimes boys behave differently than girls. Might such differences be biologically determined? Could they be culturally determined?

   - Youth culture and grown-up culture: Rules might be different among young people than among older people, and therefore we can see different reactions to a specific action depending on whether it is directed toward a young person or a grown-up. Are the differences between young and elderly people smaller than we think? Are there larger differences within the category of older people than between young and old in general?

   - Families: There may be large differences between open and hidden rules in families. Discuss which differences there may be and how to adapt to these rules when visiting a new home.

   - National and ethnic culture: Different nations and ethnic cultures have different open and hidden rules. When we come to a new nation or culture, we have to learn new cues or we could be regarded as impolite or rude. Might there be larger differences between the people in a given ethnic culture than between people in general?

   - Subcultures: Different subcultures may have different rules within a larger nation or group.

2. Choose from among the following or make up your own exercises according to the capabilities of participants.

### Exercise 1

Read and discuss the following story:

Some new neighbors have moved into the neighborhood. They have moved here from another country and are having a big party for the young daughter's birthday. Sara has been invited and, on arriving, she sees the food arranged on the table buffet style. She is encouraged to take a plate and fill it up with food. She notices some men sitting at the table without plates, and she laughs and asks them if they aren't hungry. In a few minutes the wives and mothers of the men are busy filling plates with food. They take the plates over to each man. Afterward, they go back and give the men something to drink. The men retreat outside in a group and are sitting around a cooking stove. Sara goes over to introduce herself, and the men look down and avoid eye contact. Sara feels uncomfortable and returns to the house. Sara is handed a plate of chilies, and the women look at her with smiles and encouragement. They nod her toward the chiles. She watches other guests take a chili and then spit it out and everyone laughs. Sara takes a chili and puts it part way into her mouth; it is very hot, and she spits it out. Everyone laughs and pats her on the back, and she feels a part of the group. Then everyone goes outside where there is a huge piñata shaped like a donkey; it is beautiful—pink and white. The children are taken out and lined up. They walk up to the piñata and take a swat. After each swat, the child is nudged to the back of the line. One child tries to take a second swat; the child is kept out for two turns. Once the piñata is broken, there is laughing and yelling, and no one stops all the children from tearing the piñata up and getting all the candy.

## Exercise 2

Read and discuss this puzzle:

A father and son were out driving and had a crash. Father and son were badly injured. The son was taken to the emergency room at the hospital. The doctor comes to examine the boy. The doctor exclaims, "Oh my god! It's my son." Who is the doctor? (Answer: The boy's mother.)

## Exercise 3

Read and discuss the following story:

A Norwegian tourist in Thailand sees a cute little girl. The tourist goes over and pats the girl on the head. He thinks she's cute and wants to let the girl and her mother know. The mother and the girl find this it insulting. Why? (Answer: In Thailand it is an insult to touch somebody's head. )

Select and show appropriate video clips and let the participants identify cultural misunderstandings. (A good example is *Shrek 2* where Shrek is having dinner with the king and queen.)

3. Identify the need: Discuss and record reasons it may be important to be able to identify cultural differences.

4. Identify situations where the concept is important: Discuss and record situations in which it is important to identify cultural differences. Note the names of group members as they make suggestions.

## Steps 2-9

*After the presentation of the topic of the day, the session follows the usual structure (see pages 30–33 for procedure details).*

- **STEP 2:** Facilitators present one situation. (See suggested role-plays, Appendix B.)

- **STEP 3:** Participants analyze the situation. (Display the Social Perception Training Reflection Form, Appendix C.)

- **STEP 4:** Participants suggest alternative ways of continuing the role-play.

- **STEP 5:** Participants choose one solution.

- **STEP 6:** Participants role-play the chosen solution.

- **STEP 7:** Facilitators and participants conduct feedback round.

- **STEP 8:** Facilitators and participants repeat Steps 4–7.

- **STEP 9:** Facilitators assign homework.

*Hand out copies of the Social Perception Training Log as homework and answer any questions. Briefly review the session, conduct a friendship round or other group ritual, describe the topic for the next session, and recognize participants for their efforts.*

# SESSION 5
# Setting Events

## AIM OF THE SESSION

To make participants aware of factors that influence our mood and thus lead us to react more negatively and to encourage mindfulness of the fact that others may have had a bad day and therefore need extra consideration

## THEORETICAL BACKGROUND

Setting events are background variables that indirectly alter an interaction. Thus, if an interaction fails or produces a different outcome than expected, this may be due to preinteraction stimulus conditions (setting events) rather than to stimulus conditions that arise during the interaction or skills used in the interaction. To correctly interpret one's own and others' behavior in interactions, one needs to understand the concept of setting events.

For example, Whaler and Graves (1983) have described how mothers' low socio-economic status and frequent coercive exchanges with relatives and social support staff negatively affect parent training outcomes. Chandler and colleagues (Chandler, Fowler, & Lubeck, 1992) have assessed the impact of some setting events on children's social play and found that child interaction covaries with teacher presence and teacher direction in the play situation. Fox and Conroy (1995) have described how a student who has had a fight with a peer on the school bus on the way to school may be more likely to demonstrate disruptive behavior in the classroom.

Setting events may be of an environmental, social, or physiological nature. *Environmental setting events* include, among others, crowded conditions, barren environment, noise level, heat/cold, time of day, type of music played, and physical layout of the environment. *Social setting events* include, for example, minor or major life changes, a previous fight with peers, previous negative social interactions, ongoing family discord, the presence of certain individuals, and losing a game. *Physiological setting events* may include agitation due to emotions or physiological conditions (e.g., menstruation, changes in or side effects of medication, sleep disturbances, pain, allergies, infections, hunger/thirst, and physical or mental illnesses).

Setting events thus influence how we deal with a provocation (Bijou & Baer, 1961). Examples of events exerting an influence on people's reactions to social challenges at the personal level include the effects of sleep deprivation (O'Reilly, 1995), caffeine intake (Carr, Reeve, & Magito-McLaughlin, 1996), and prior viewing of videos with violent content. Increasing attention has been directed toward the effects of alcohol (Anderson & Dill, 2000) and drugs (Anderson & Bushman, 2002) on violent behavior.

Other events take place at the interpersonal level. In crowds and in other situations where the participants have little room (personal space), people express emotional behavior more rapidly and powerfully than they do in less crowded situations. In a building where there is no clear exit and the existence of some perceived threat (e.g., smoke billowing into a room or a sudden loud noise), people resort more quickly to aggressive and threatening behavior. Many adolescents with behavioral problems tend to put the blame for their aggressive behavior on external circumstances, whereas they view other people's aggression as being a permanent character trait in the individuals concerned (Novaco & Welsh, 1989). These youth show little understanding for the possibility that other people may be in a bad mood or that some external event has influenced their state of mind.

To interpret a situation as correctly as possible, it is important to think through any possible background variables/events both for oneself and one's partner in the interaction. The ability to reflect upon background variables/events that may give rise to different emotional states is closely connected to the concept of empathy.

In this session, it may be useful to consider background variables/events that make us more positive and able to deal better with external triggers. Examples include receiving praise for making an effort, talking with a person with experience of adapting to new situations, seeing a film about immigrants who adjust well to their new environments, and taking a break in order to relax or refresh oneself.

# PROCEDURE

*Welcome the group and, if desired, conduct an opening ritual and share an optical illusion. Remind participants of rules, review the previous session, and discuss the previous session's homework.*

## Step 1

1. Identify the concept or topic of the day: Define and discuss the concept of setting events. Ask participants what they think the concept means and record the group's suggestions on a whole-group display. If necessary, paraphrase:

   > Often we bring experiences, thoughts, emotions, or physiological status (like pain or tiredness) from one situation to another. These setting events influence the way we think and act, even if they are not directly connected to the situation we are in. For example, if you are tired, you might have a "shorter fuse" or less tolerance for mistakes and you thus might react differently than if you had had a great night's sleep.

2. Choose from among the following or make up your own exercises according to the capabilities of participants.

### Exercise 1

Ask the participants to describe times they want someone to understand them better. Consider also situations in which individual participants should have understood others better. Write these situations on the board. Point out that it is important to think about the consequences in situations where you are easily provoked and learn that you should be careful in such situations. The second point is that you must take into account and respect the fact that others may have had a bad day.

### Exercise 2

Read aloud the following situations and have the participants discuss the possible background variables/events in each case:

- You call your girlfriend, and she answers gruffly, "What do you want?"
- A mother comes home from work. School bags, clothes, and socks lie strewn across the hall. She starts to cry.
- A father comes home from work, whistling happily. The mother is getting more and more sullen.
- Tracy, 14 years old, is squabbling with her kid sister, Sally, about trifles.
- The teacher asks Jim to take out his math book. Jim says, "Go to hell!"
- Steve has asked Liz out to the movies. She goes with him but is in a bad mood.

3. Identify possible situations where the concept is important. Record the situations group members suggest in which it is important to understand that there may be various reasons others react as they do and also times you would like others to understand you better. Write the names of participants who suggest these situations.

4. Identify the need: Record reasons it may be important to know about the concept of setting events. Also discuss the idea that if you yourself have had a bad day, it is no reason to behave badly toward others.

## Steps 2-9

*After the presentation of the topic of the day, the session follows the usual structure (see pages 30–33 for procedure details).*

- **STEP 2:** Facilitators present one situation. (See suggested role-plays, Appendix B.)
- **STEP 3:** Participants analyze the situation. (Display the Social Perception Training Reflection Form, Appendix C.)
- **STEP 4:** Participants suggest alternative ways of continuing the role-play.
- **STEP 5:** Participants choose one solution.
- **STEP 6:** Participants role-play the chosen solution.
- **STEP 7:** Facilitators and participants conduct feedback round.
- **STEP 8:** Facilitators and participants repeat Steps 4–7 as time allows.
- **STEP 9:** Facilitators assign homework.

*Hand out copies of the Social Perception Training Log as homework and answer any questions. Briefly review the session, conduct a friendship round or other group ritual, describe the topic for the next session, and recognize participants for their efforts.*

# SESSION 6
# Thoughts, Feelings, Body Signals, and Actions

## AIM OF THE SESSION

To help participants understand that what we think about a situation influences how we feel and which body signals and reactions we have, as well as to promote awareness that our feelings about a situation may interfere with how we think and react and that our reactions in a situation may interfere with how we feel and think

## THEORETICAL BACKGROUND

How we interpret and react to a social situation is associated with our feelings and body signals. Our feelings or mood will affect not only how we think in a given situation, but also our body signals. When we feel sad, we automatically access our thinking, and the sadness is also reflected in our facial expression. The reverse also applies. When we adjust our body signals—for instance by straightening our back or smiling—these changes can produce changes in feelings consistent with the body signals. Emotional reactions are often our primary responses to changes in social situations, and we have a tendency to make cognitive interpretations in accordance with or reaction to our feelings. However, our emotions can be influenced by other factors that we are not aware of and are in many cases not trustworthy. One example is how fear may influence the tendency to feel attraction toward a female passenger on a plane (Svartdal, 2011). It is therefore important that we find different ways of thinking about what is going on in a specific situation and not rely solely on our first emotional reactions. How we interpret a situation and therefore think about it hugely influences our feelings and therefore our body signals and actions. Together, these factors strongly influence how we react.

The goal of this session is to make participants aware of how these factors influence our reactions. If we can manage to think positively, this will result in positive actions toward other people. Those participants who have had, or are having, Anger Control Training can be asked whether they see a similarity between this session's content and the anger control chain. Note that the tendency to interpret signals negatively in unclear situations is one of the most typical attributions for individuals with behavioral problems (Waldman, 1996). The way we view a given situation is also connected to our expectations of how we *believe* other people to be (see Rosenthal & Jacobsen, 1968). Such preconceived conceptions tend to be inflexible because we get a false confirmation that something really is the way we believe it to be. This phenomenon, known as a self-fulfilling prophecy, happens more or less subconsciously (Darley & Fazio, 1980).

## PROCEDURE

*Welcome the group and, if desired, conduct an opening ritual and share an optical illusion. Remind participants of rules, review the previous session, and discuss the previous session's homework.*

### Step 1

1. Identify the concept or topic of the day: Define and discuss the relationship among thoughts, feelings, body signals, and actions. Give each participant a copy of the Situation Analysis Form and refer to it to help you explain. If necessary, paraphrase:

   > How we interpret a situation impacts our feelings, body signals, and also how we further react. Sometimes our feelings and body signals come first, and we might interpret a situation through how we react emotionally, rather than basing our actions on a cognitive appraisal of the situation. Changes in one of these factors will thus have an impact on the others.

2. Work through an example, showing the thoughts, feelings, body signals, and actions on a whole-group display of the diagram:

   > Situation: Your friend is better at the guitar than you are (an area that is important for your self-definition).

   a. What are your *thoughts* about this? I'm glad I've got a friend who's good at the guitar. It's nice to have a friend that I can maybe learn from.

   b. Thoughts like these influence our *feelings* about this person and about playing the guitar in general. With such an interpretation, the feeling will probably be gladness.

   c. We recognize our *body signals,* which reflect the thoughts and corresponding feelings. Ask participants for examples of body signals that reflect these thoughts and feelings (relaxed muscles, calm breathing).

   d. Our thoughts, feelings, and body signals then affect the *actions* we choose. Ask participants for examples (ask to play guitar with him, practice more).

3. Then ask participants if they can think of different thoughts they might have in this situation and have them identify the feeling, body signals, and actions related to this new thought. For example:

   a. Thought: He just likes to show off all the time.

   b. Feelings: Jealousy, anger

   c. Body signals: Heart pumping, tension in the stomach

d. Action: Avoid him, stop playing guitar and start another hobby

4. Choose from among the following exercises. Provide additional copies of the diagram as needed.

### Exercise 1

Situation: Ann is very good at handball and scored 10 goals, while Rachel scored 5. Ann was praised by their trainer.

Have half of the group first write down different *thoughts* on the Situation Analysis Form and then fill in the other sections, reflecting on how the different thoughts could influence Ann's feelings, body signals, and actions.

Have the other half first fill out different *feelings* that Rachel might have brought with her into the handball game and then reflect on whether the different emotional states would affect her thoughts, body signals, and actions.

### Exercise 2

Situation: Freddy is looking at Susan. Susan notices this.

Have participants fill out the diagram with a thought Susan might be having and then add the related feelings, body signals, and actions.

On another form, have the group fill out what Freddy might be thinking and then add Freddy's related feelings, body signals, and actions.

### Exercise 3

Situation: Liz knocks into Chuck in the corridor.

What is Chuck thinking, and how could these thoughts affect his subsequent feelings, signals and actions?

### Exercise 4

Situation: Ken has just got a new computer. Tommy has wanted a new computer for over a year.

Have participants fill out the diagram with a thought Ken might be having and then add the related feelings, body signals, and actions.

On another form, have the group fill out what Tommy might be thinking and then add Freddy's related feelings, body signals, and actions.

5. Identify specific situations in which it is important to consider this topic. Write down participants' suggestions.

6. Specify the need to know about this concept. Why is it important to know about our own attributions of a situation?

## Steps 2-9

*After the presentation of the topic of the day, the session follows the usual structure (see pages 30–33 for procedure details).*

- **STEP 2:** Facilitators present one situation. (See suggested role-plays, Appendix B.)

- **STEP 3:** Participants analyze the situation. (Display the Social Perception Training Reflection Form, Appendix C.)
- **STEP 4:** Participants suggest alternative ways of continuing the role-play.
- **STEP 5:** Participants choose one solution.
- **STEP 6:** Participants role-play the chosen solution.
- **STEP 7:** Facilitators and participants conduct feedback round.
- **STEP 8:** Facilitators and participants repeat Steps 4–7 as time allows.
- **STEP 9:** Facilitators assign homework.

   *Hand out copies of the Social Perception Training Log as homework and answer any questions. Briefly review the session, conduct a friendship round or other group ritual, describe the topic for the next session, and recognize participants for their efforts.*

# Situation Analysis Form

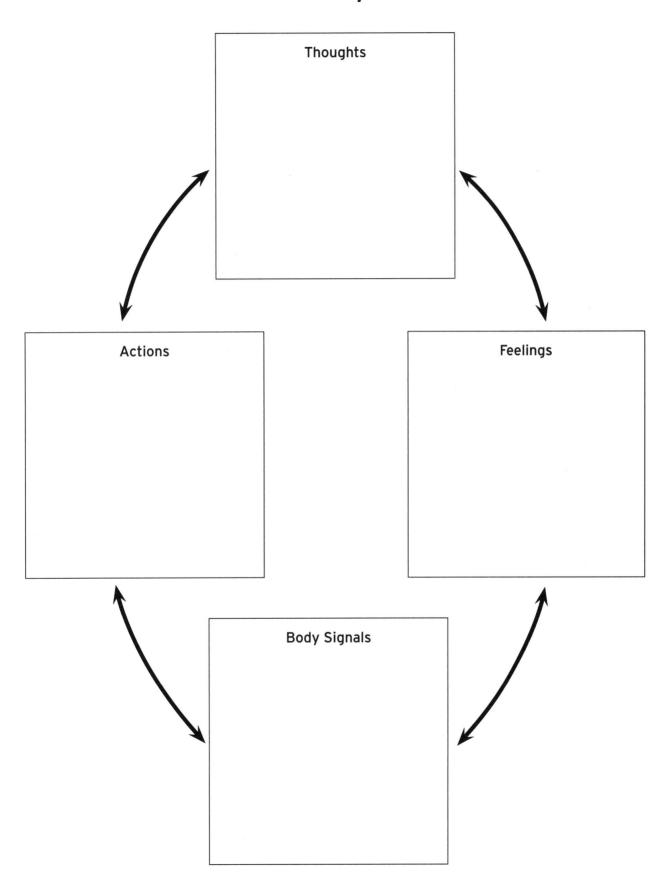

# SESSION 7
# Interpreting Others' Intentions

## AIM OF THE SESSION

To help participants reflect on different ways of interpreting the intentions of other people

## THEORETICAL BASIS

An understanding of verbal and nonverbal messages will to a great extent enable us also to understand the intentions or goals behind what another person says or does. However, we do not always speak or act rationally; we often hide our feelings, and in many cases we "test the water" by adopting a consciously ambiguous way of reacting. Imagine a teenage boy who deliberately bumps into a girl. He may fancy her but is too embarrassed to say so directly, or he wants to send out feelers to see her reaction without losing face at the outset. An important distinction is whether we interpret the other's intention as *internal* (dispositional) or *external* (situational) (Heider, 1958). Think of another example: A father is yelling at his daughter. This could be interpreted with regard to the father himself (e.g., he's crazy, he's had a bad day). However, we might also try to find the reason in the situation (e.g., she was crossing a dangerous road and he had to rush and stop her).

As described in the previous session, antisocial youth and individuals with aggression problems tend to misinterpret other people's signals as hostile in ambiguous situations. Often these young people have experienced physical or mental/psychological harm by parents or other members of their intimate network and will in a new situation have a tendency to believe that other people they meet also will harm them. Early abuse is thus a predictor of aggressive behavior in kindergarten (Dodge, Price, Bachorowski, & Newman, 1990). Another important factor for hostile intent may also be how the person perceives himself or herself. When he or she feels of low worth, this attribution may lead to a belief that also others look at the person in the same way. This interpretation will in turn cause oversensitivity to signs in others that seem to confirm this and thus create aggression. Thoughts like "He is out to get me," "I am always being picked on," and so forth may be a well-established tendency, and such interpretations can readily become habitual. Many situations are also unclear because we and our partners in interaction perceive things differently, represent different cultures, or transfer our own attribution pattern to others. The most important tool to use when a situation is ambiguous and we are unsure of the intention is of course to ask questions. This should be a thread through both this and other sessions. It is also important to teach participants to be aware of the dangers of having the opposite perspective—one can think too well of people. Sometimes people are not friendly, and their intention may be to harm you. As in other sessions, clarification is needed if you are unsure of what is happening.

## PROCEDURE

*Facilitators welcome the group and, if desired, conduct an opening ritual and share an optical illusion. They remind participants of rules, review the previous session, and discuss the previous session's homework.*

### Step 1

1. Identify the concept or topic of the day: Define and discuss the concept of intentions. Ask participants what they think the concept means and record the group's suggestions on a whole-group display. If necessary, paraphrase:

   > An intention can be defined as what you or another wish to achieve in a certain situation. For example, you might want to be kind, to get something from the situation, to flirt, to bribe someone to do something, to get revenge, to humiliate someone, or to get recognition.

2. Explain that people can have very different intentions for performing the same action. For example:
   - Giving a compliment ("bribing," being nice, flirting, hoping for something in return)
   - Helping (showing off, being helpful, hoping for something in return)
   - Giving a present ("bribing," being nice)
   - Talking about one's car (being proud, boasting, humiliating someone who has a cheaper car)
   - Bumping into you (by accident, on purpose, fancies you)
   - Looking at your girlfriend/boyfriend, smiling and nodding (knows her/him already, wants to chat her/him up)

   Point out that it is generally better to assume that people have positive intentions.

3. Role-play or, if possible, show a video clip of a situation illustrating an ambiguous intention. Elicit various interpretations from the participants. Based on the following list, ask participants for alternative interpretations. For example: "He/she isn't really out to get me," "He wasn't aware it was my turn," "He just picked on the nearest person—it happened to be me." To enhance understanding of alternative interpretations, list participants' responses as they generate them.

4. Choose from among the following or make up your own exercises according to the capabilities of participants.

#### Exercise 1

Oscar is taking Linda's backpack. Try to figure out different intentions that Oscar may have.

**Exercise 2**

What might be these people's intentions?

- Helen is reviewing for the math test. She's got stuck on one of the questions. Her teacher is too busy to help her. Sue, who's top of the class in math, sees Helen's plight and goes over to her and asks if she can help.

- Tracy goes up to Hannah during recess. Tracy tells Hannah to keep her hands off Ken. Ken danced with Hannah at the youth club. Ken is going out with Celine, who is in Tracy's class.

- Robert tells about the time John was going to play the guitar in public and had forgotten to put his guitar in the guitar case. Everyone laughs. John is also present.

5. Identify specific situations in which is it important to consider the other person's intention. Write down participants' suggestions.

6. Specify the need to know about this concept. Ask participants why it is important to learn more about different intentions in a situation and write down their responses.

## Steps 2-9

*After the presentation of the topic of the day, the session follows the usual structure (see pages 30–33 for procedure details).*

- **STEP 2:** Facilitators present one situation. (See suggested role-plays, Appendix B.)

- **STEP 3:** Participants analyze the situation. (Display the Social Perception Training Reflection Form, Appendix C.)

- **STEP 4:** Participants suggest alternative ways of continuing the role-play.

- **STEP 5:** Participants choose one solution.

- **STEP 6:** Participants role-play the chosen solution.

- **STEP 7:** Facilitators and participants conduct feedback round.

- **STEP 8:** Facilitators and participants repeat Steps 4–7 as time allows.

- **STEP 9:** Facilitators assign homework.

*Hand out copies of the Social Perception Training Log as homework and answer any questions. Briefly review the session, conduct a friendship round or other group ritual, describe the topic for the next session, and recognize participants for their efforts.*

# SESSION 8
# Cognitive Distortions

## AIM OF THE SESSION

To assist participants in identifying typical cognitive distortions that might contribute to a false perception of a social situation

## THEORETICAL BASIS

It is not always external events that determine how we interpret a situation. Our interpretation is often based on what we think about these events. Burns (1980) has described various misinterpretations that represent typical cognitive distortions:

1. All or nothing thinking: You see things in black and white categories. If your performance falls short of perfect, you see yourself as a total failure.

2. Overgeneralization: You see a single negative event as a never-ending pattern of defeat.

3. Mental filter: You pick out a single negative detail and dwell on it exclusively so that your vision of all reality becomes darkened, like the drop of ink that discolors the entire beaker of water.

4. Disqualifying the positive: You reject positive experiences by insisting they "don't count" for some reason or other. In this way you can maintain a negative belief that is contradicted by your everyday experiences.

5. Jumping to conclusions: You make negative interpretations, even though there are definite facts that convincingly do not support your conclusions.

6. Magnification (catastrophizing) or minimization: You exaggerate the importance of things (e.g., your own goof-up) or you inappropriately devalue things (e.g., your own desirable qualities or another person's achievements). This is also called the "binocular trick."

7. Emotional reasoning: You assume that your negative emotions necessarily reflect the way things really are: "I feel it, so it must be true."

8. "Should" statements: You try to motivate yourself with "shoulds" and "shouldn'ts," as though you have to be punished before you can be expected to do anything. "Musts" and "oughts" are also offenders. The emotional consequence is guilt. When you direct "should" statements toward others, you feel anger, frustration, and resentment when they do not act in accordance with *your* expectations.

9. Labeling and mislabeling: This is an extreme form of overgeneralization. Instead of describing your error, you attach a negative label to yourself: "I'm a loser." When someone else's behavior rubs you the wrong way, you attach a negative label to that person: "He's a damn jerk." Mislabeling involves describing an event with language that is highly colored and emotionally loaded. The language is also formulated in terms of permanent characteristics and not limited to specific events.

10. Personalization: You see yourself as the cause of some negative external event, over which you are in fact not primarily responsible.

The Moral Reasoning component of ART focuses on what are known as self-centered cognitive distortions (Barriga, Morrison, Liau, & Gibbs, 2000; Gibbs, Potter, & Goldstein, 1995; Glick & Gibbs, 2011), considered typical of young people with behavioral problems. Such distortions are viewed as defense mechanisms whose function is to legitimize wrong actions. The actions are primarily considered from the youth's own point of view. In other words, the youth is so concerned about his or her own opinions, expectations, needs, and rights that he or she scarcely thinks about, or completely rejects, any justifiable points of view the other person may have. Self-centeredness is the primary distorting factor, from which stem three secondary cognitive distortions, whose function is to rationalize the egocentric way of thinking.

1. Self-centered: For example, "I am stealing because I am a girl who steals."

2. Minimizing: For example, "Everybody tells lies" and "We were only messing with him."

3. Blaming others: For example, "It was her fault," "The cops are after him," "He should have had a burglar alarm," and "She told me to do it."

4. Assuming the worst: For example, "I might as well hit her first, before she hits me," "Me hurting you is better than you hurting me!" "I might as well steal it—if I don't, some other guy will."

To avoid making the session too complicated, especially for younger participants, facilitators should limit the number of cognitive distortions. We recommend emphasizing the preceding distortions (self-centered, minimizing, blaming others, assuming the worst) and perhaps including a few others if they are relevant for the participants involved.

# PROCEDURE

*Facilitators welcome the group and, if desired, conduct a friendship round or other opening ritual and share an optical illusion. They remind participants of rules, review the previous session, and discuss the previous session's homework.*

## Step 1

1. Identify the concept or topic of the day: Define and discuss cognitive distortions. Ask participants what they think the concept means and write suggestions on a whole-group display. If necessary, paraphrase the idea that cognitive distortions are arguments we often use when we want to justify actions we actually think are not right.

2. Conduct the following exercise or make up your own exercises according to the capabilities of participants.

### Exercise

Give each participant a copy of the Cognitive Distortions handout and an imaginary remote control (made of cardboard or paper); then role-play or read aloud the following situations. Have participants press a button on the remote control and say, "Stop" to signal that they have observed a cognitive distortion. Then they identify one of the cognitive distortions. (Have them identify the error to the best of their ability.)

- Steve sat bragging to his friends about the break-ins he had committed: "The guy had just the kind of cell phone I've been looking for. When I see something I want, I just take it (self-centered). He seemed to have a lot of money, too, so it wouldn't be a big deal to him (minimizing). He'll probably get it back from the insurance. What the hell, it was lying on the table—if I hadn't taken it, somebody else surely would have" (assuming the worst).

- Extract from an interrogation log: "All I did was smash a beer bottle over his head (minimizing). Besides, he was more or less asking for it all evening" (blaming others).

- The burglar thought, "Who is so stupid as to leave the key in the door? It's his own fault if he's burglarized (blaming others). Anybody would have done the same" (self-centered, assuming the worst).

- Karen was in charge of preparing the Sunday dinner. Her husband complained loudly that the roast beef was too dry. Karen thought, "I'm a total failure. Everything I do turns out wrong" (assuming the worst).

- Peter said, "Besides, it wasn't my fault. I was so drunk I can't remember anything" (blaming others).

- Andrew was turned down when he asked a female colleague out to dinner. He thought, "No one will ever go out with me. I'm never going to meet anyone who likes me, who I can date" (assuming the worst).

- "Did you see how he stared at me, that jerk? Isn't it typical? People are always out to get me (assuming the worst). It's better if I hit them first."

- "I expect myself to find quick and proper solutions to any problem that pops up. If I don't, I might as well dig a hole and jump in it" (assuming the worst).

- Simon has just learned that the course he's taking has written exams. He thinks, "No, I always do poorly on written exams—I must be excused from that" (self-centered, assuming the worst).

3. Identify specific situations in which is it important to consider the use of thinking errors. Write down participants' suggestions as they generate them.

4. Specify the need to know about thinking errors. Write down participants suggestions.

### Steps 2-9

*After the presentation of the topic of the day, the session follows the usual structure (see pages 30–33 for procedure details).*

- **STEP 2:** Facilitators present one situation. (See suggested role-plays, Appendix B.)
- **STEP 3:** Participants analyze the situation. (Display the Social Perception Training Reflection Form, Appendix C.)
- **STEP 4:** Participants suggest alternative ways of continuing the role-play.
- **STEP 5:** Participants choose one solution.
- **STEP 6:** Participants role-play the chosen solution.
- **STEP 7:** Facilitators and participants conduct feedback round.
- **STEP 8:** Facilitators and participants repeat Steps 4–7 as time allows.
- **STEP 9:** Facilitators assign homework.

*Hand out copies of the Social Perception Training Log as homework and answer any questions. Briefly review the session, conduct a friendship round or other group ritual, describe the topic for the next session, and recognize participants for their efforts.*

# Cognitive Distortions

## Self-centered

Self-centered thinking means that you think your opinions and feelings are more important than the opinions and feelings of other people. It can also mean that you think only about what you want right now and do not think about how your behaviors will affect you or others in the future.

## Minimizing/mislabeling

Minimizing/mislabeling means that you think your problems or behaviors are not as wrong or harmful as they really are. You put a label on your bad behavior to make it sound OK, or you describe someone with a bad name so it will seem OK to hurt the person.

## Assuming the worst

Assuming the worst means that you think everyone is out to get you (or someone else). Assuming the worst about yourself means that you think only bad things can happen to you and you can't do anything about it. It can also mean that you think you or other people will never be able to change or improve.

## Blaming others

Blaming others means that you blame other people for harmful behavior when it is really your fault. You may think you can harm people because they treated you badly in the past. Blaming others can also mean you think your bad behavior is OK because you were in a bad mood or on drugs or alcohol.

From *Social Perception Training,* by K. K. Gundersen, B. Strømgren, & I. moynahan, © 2013, Champaign, IL: Research Press (800-519-2707, www.researchpress.com).

# SESSION 9
# Timing (Right Time and Place)

## AIM OF THE SESSION

To help participants discriminate between situations in which specific actions are and are not considered right or proper

## THEORETICAL BASIS

By *discrimination,* we mean differentiating between those situations in which a given action will lead to a desired consequence and those situations in which the action will not have the same effect. In social competence training, certain skills are practiced. But these skills are not worth much if the participants are unable to transfer them to real situations (generalization) or know in which situations to use them and when not to use them (differentiation/discrimination). In this session, the focus is on when we should employ certain skills, such as starting a conversation and taking the initiative to play, and when we should choose to interact in another way: ask for help, give a compliment, and so forth. When do we tell a person she has beautiful eyes, and when do we definitely not? When should we ask for help, and when should we wait?

The same fluency-based training format described in Session 2 (see Figure 5) may also be used to prepare participants to decide whether it is the right time and place to take a certain action (e.g., to try out the Skillstreaming skill of Starting a Conversation). Which social cues indicate yes, and which cues indicate no? Arrange brief role-plays involving the facilitators and the other participants. Again, the trick is to start with simple vignettes with clear depictions of "open to contact" or "not open to contact" and gradually increase the complexity of the situation and the ambiguity of openness/no openness during the repetitions, depending on how many correct answers the participant gives. A further refinement may be to have facilitators and participants alter their social cues contingent upon the participant's performance. If the vignette is displaying "not open to contact," these cues may be altered toward more openness if the participant approaches in a socially acceptable manner (e.g. slowly, without anger signals, smiling, etc.).

## PROCEDURE

*Facilitators welcome the group and, if desired, conduct an opening ritual and share an optical illusion. They remind participants of rules, review the previous session, and discuss the previous session's homework.*

**Step 1**

1. Identify the concept or topic of the day: Define and discuss the concept of timing. Ask participants what they think the concept means and record the group's suggestions on a whole-group display. If necessary, paraphrase:

> Timing means judging and acting when it is the right time and place for an action. It is important to distinguish between when our words and actions help to gain a positive result or avoid a negative result and when it is best to wait or even *not* say or do something that interrupts, delays, or hinders achieving a positive result.

2. Show a video clip, if possible, or role-play an example like the following: Ms. Smith, the teacher, is out of the classroom, and Brian, one of the students, sees Victor take some money from Ms. Smith's handbag.

**Ms. Smith:** (Arriving back) Thank you for waiting. Now you can take out your math books.

**Brian:** (Shouting) Ms. Smith, Ms. Smith! Victor took money out of your handbag when you were out. I saw him!

**Victor:** (At the top of his voice) I didn't! You're lying!

**Ms. Smith:** Thank you for telling me, Brian. (She looks in her handbag, and sees that her money is missing, and says) Victor, go straight to the principal's office and tell him what you've done.

**Victor:** (Clenches his fist at Brian) You're gonna die after school today.

Ask the following questions:

- Was it right of Victor to take the money?
- Did Brian choose the right time and place to tell Ms. Smith?
- Could Brian have been more discreet, and if so, how?

3. Choose from among the following or make up your own exercises according to the capabilities of participants.

### Exercise 1

Give each participant a copy of the Right Time and Place? handout and ask participants whether it's the right time in each case for the child to ask her or his mother a question. Ask for the reasons and perhaps also inquire as to what the children should do until it's a more suitable time to ask.

### Exercise 2

Provide copies of the Good or Bad Timing? handout, then read out each of the following numbered sentences and tell the students to check "good" or "bad" to describe the timing. Consider including other examples relevant to the age group of the participants and their particular problems.

4. In which specific situations is it important to consider the use of right time and place? Record participants' suggestions.

5. Specify the need to know about this concept. Why is it important to know more about timing?

## Steps 2-9

*After the presentation of the topic of the day, the session follows the usual structure (see pages 30–33 for procedure details).*

- **STEP 2:** Facilitators present one situation. (See suggested role-plays, Appendix B.)
- **STEP 3:** Participants analyze the situation. (Display the Social Perception Training Reflection Form, Appendix C.)
- **STEP 4:** Participants suggest alternative ways of continuing the role-play.
- **STEP 5:** Participants choose one solution.
- **STEP 6:** Participants role-play the chosen solution.
- **STEP 7:** Facilitators and participants conduct feedback round.
- **STEP 8:** Facilitators and participants repeat Steps 4–7 as time allows.
- **STEP 9:** Facilitators assign homework.

*Hand out copies of the Social Perception Training Log as homework and answer any questions. Briefly review the session, conduct a friendship round or other group ritual, describe the topic for the next session, and recognize participants for their efforts.*

# Right Time and Place?

# Good or Bad Timing?

|  | Good | Bad |
|---|:---:|:---:|
| 1. John asks Carl if he wants to play soccer just after Carl has sprained his ankle. | ❏ | ❏ |
| 2. Richard asks his brother for help with his homework just as his brother is about to make a parachute jump. | ❏ | ❏ |
| 3. Ruth wins $100 in a lottery and calls her friends at 3 A.M. to tell them. | ❏ | ❏ |
| 4. Susan wants the latest Donkeyboys hit and asks for it two days before her birthday. | ❏ | ❏ |
| 5. Tommy asks the teacher for help with math while the teacher's talking to the principal. | ❏ | ❏ |
| 6. Rolf asks if he can leave the classroom for a drink of water just as the teacher is starting the lesson. | ❏ | ❏ |
| 7. Robert asks if he can play ball with some others just when they've finished a game. | ❏ | ❏ |
| 8. Barbara asks to borrow Mary's calculator just after the teacher has gotten angry with Mary. | ❏ | ❏ |
| 9. Steve asks Ken for a favor right after Ken falls off his bike and bruises his knees. | ❏ | ❏ |
| 10. Carol asks her mother for a new bike just after the old one has been stolen because Carol left it at the movies and forgot to lock it. | ❏ | ❏ |
| 11. Ellen asks for a later curfew right after her birthday. | ❏ | ❏ |
| 12. Ellen asks for a later curfew after coming home on time every day for three weeks. | ❏ | ❏ |

From *Social Perception Training,* by K. K. Gundersen, B. Strømgren, & I. moynahan, © 2013, Champaign, IL: Research Press (800-519-2707, www.researchpress.com).

# SESSION 10
# Consequences (If-Then)

## AIM OF THE SESSION

To increase the participants' understanding of alternative choices and the consequences of those choices

## THEORETICAL BASIS

Our actions always lead to some kind of consequences. If we take playing the piano as an example, we can imagine a number of different consequences: I play piano and someone praises me for it; I play piano to stop my mother nagging at me to practice. In both these cases, the consequence is that I carry on playing. These two forms of consequences are called, respectively, positive and negative reinforcement. However, we can also imagine that my piano teacher is always getting annoyed with me or that I can't play football with my friends if I take the piano lessons. In these two cases, the consequence is likely to be that I won't carry on playing. The consequences can arise from myself (I enjoy playing) or from others (I get praise). They can also be short term or long term. I can put up with the boredom of practicing scales because I want to be a famous pianist one day. We are also influenced by consequences for other people. This is known as vicarious reinforcement (Bandura, 1977b). In many cases, we are confronted with a choice where one alternative leads to a short-term gain (I take a wallet and get money) but also leads to a long-term negative consequence (If I get found out, I'll be known as a thief).

Children and youth with behavioral problems generate, on the whole, fewer prosocial skills in stressful situations (Hollin, 1999), consider fewer alternatives before deciding on an action, and rely more on internalized reactions, which often include aggression (Veneziano & Veneziano, 1988). The choice of response entails primarily an assessment of the various consequences that may follow from the different alternative actions. In a stressful situation, such an assessment is less likely. Considering the possible consequences of alternative choices in situations where adolescents typically find themselves will help us conduct a "preanalysis" that can be beneficial when choices have to be made in real situations. A useful approach is to separate the consequences into social (exclusion, bad reputation), legal (fine, imprisonment), and physical harm (to others or self). It is also helpful to consider unintended consequences; if you are especially unlucky, the person who is going to give you a job happens to find out what you've done.

# PROCEDURE

*Facilitators welcome the group and, if desired, conduct an opening ritual and share an optical illusion. They remind participants of rules, review the previous session, and discuss the previous session's homework.*

## Step 1

1. Identify the concept or topic of the day: Define and discuss the concept of consequences. Ask the group what they think the concept means. Write the group's suggestions on a whole-group display and help participants get the concept right. If necessary, explain that consequences are what happen after an action, right away or after some time has gone by. Consequences might be good or bad.

2. Conduct the following exercise or make up your own exercises according to the capabilities of participants.

### Exercise

Divide the group into two. Give each group a Consequences Situation Card. Have the groups analyze the situation and find the best alternative. They then role-play the situation and alternative for the other participants, followed by a discussion about why this choice was the best for all concerned. Help participants interpret the situation in the light of previous sessions.

3. Identify specific situations in which it is important to consider consequences. Record participants' ideas.

4. Specify the need to know about this concept.

## Steps 2-9

*After the presentation of the topic of the day, the session follows the usual structure (see pages 30–33 for procedure details).*

- **STEP 2:** Facilitators present one situation. (See suggested role-plays, Appendix B.)
- **STEP 3:** Participants analyze the situation. (Display the Social Perception Training Reflection Form, Appendix C.)
- **STEP 4:** Participants suggest alternative ways of continuing the role-play.
- **STEP 5:** Participants choose one solution.
- **STEP 6:** Participants role-play the chosen solution.
- **STEP 7:** Facilitators and participants conduct feedback round.
- **STEP 8:** Facilitators and participants repeat Steps 4–7 as time allows.
- **STEP 9:** Facilitators assign homework.

    *Hand out copies of the Social Perception Training Log as homework and answer any questions. Briefly review the session, conduct a friendship round or other group ritual, describe the topic for the next session, and recognize participants for their efforts.*

# Consequences Situation Cards

## Situation 1

Your girlfriend's older brother comes when you're home alone and tells you to hide a bottle of whisky for him.

WHAT WILL HAPPEN IF YOU . . .

| Say he can hide it in your room himself? | Say yes but pour the contents down the sink and throw away the bottle? | Say yes but sell the whisky to someone else? | Say no because your parents will find it? |
| --- | --- | --- | --- |
| Suggest that he ask someone else? | Say yes but tell your parents? | | |

## Situation 2

Your boyfriend asks if you want to go with him and break into a summer house in the woods.

WHAT WILL HAPPEN IF YOU . . .

| Think it sounds exciting and go with him? | Say you can't go because you're afraid of the dark? | Say no because you don't want to break the law? | Say yes and suggest taking along all your friends? |
| --- | --- | --- | --- |
| Say yes but then call the police? | Say that you'd rather do something more fun? | Say no and explain the consequences of breaking the law? | Pretend you don't understand what he's saying? |

## Situation 3

You are in a shopping mall with some friends, and a foreign-looking boy smiles and says hello to your girlfriend.

WHAT WILL HAPPEN IF YOU . . .

| Tell him to go away? | Go up to him with your friends and threaten to beat him up? | Go up to him with your girlfriend and talk to him? | Pretend you didn't see it? |
| --- | --- | --- | --- |
| Give your girlfriend a kiss? | Tell your friends about it? | Threaten your girlfriend to "keep away from other boys"? | Ask if he'd like to join you? |

From *Social Perception Training*, by K. K. Gundersen, B. Strømgren, & I. moynahan, © 2013, Champaign, IL: Research Press (800-519-2707, www.researchpress.com).

**Situation 4**

You see a man who is drunk getting into a car, about to drive off.

WHAT WILL HAPPEN IF YOU . . .

| Run over to the man to stop him? | Shout to him that he must get out of the car? | Pretend you haven't noticed he's drunk? | Call the police? |
|---|---|---|---|
| Stand in front of the car, waving your arms? | Call home to tell your family what's happening? | Walk over to the car and ask the man politely not to drive? | Turn around and walk in the opposite direction? |

**Situation 5**

You are in tenth grade and see some students making fun of an eighth-grade girl.

WHAT WILL HAPPEN IF YOU . . .

| Pretend you haven't seen it? | Stand close by to watch? | Bring your friends so you can watch together? | Tell the teacher on duty? |
|---|---|---|---|
| Don't tell anyone about it until you get home? | Go up to them and tell them it's unacceptable? | Start making fun of her with the others? | Wait until after school, then contact the girl to find out if she needs any help? |

**Situation 6**

You see an old lady who has slipped and fallen on the ice.

WHAT WILL HAPPEN IF YOU . . .

| Pretend you didn't see it and walk another way? | Call the police to get help? | Go over to her and ask if she needs help? | Call an ambulance? |
|---|---|---|---|
| Get scared and start crying? | Call home to ask what to do? | Call your friends? | Look around to see if anyone else has seen it, then run away? |

## Situation 7

In a shop, you are waiting at the checkout when some youths bump into you so that you fall against a man.

WHAT WILL HAPPEN IF YOU . . .

| Get scared and start crying? | Turn around and shout at the ones who pushed you? | Act as if nothing had happened? | Say sorry and explain what happened? |
|---|---|---|---|
| Start to laugh out loud? | Call a friend and tell him that the man in front has weird clothes? | Put down your shopping and storm out of the shop? | Push back? |

## Situation 8

You live in an institution, and a youth asks you to keep the night staff occupied so he can sneak out at night.

WHAT WILL HAPPEN IF YOU . . .

| Help him get out? | Tell him to ask someone else? | Tell the staff? | Help him but tell the staff afterward? |
|---|---|---|---|
| Tell him that you'll tell the staff? | Try to persuade him not to sneak out? | Suggest he try to come to an agreement with the adults about permission to leave? | Pretend you didn't hear what he asked you to do? |

## Situation 9

You find a wallet on the sidewalk.

WHAT WILL HAPPEN IF YOU . . .

| Pick it up quickly and put it in your pocket? | Pretend you didn't see it? | Hide it and call a friend? | Hand it in to the police? |
|---|---|---|---|
| Take it home and give it to adults who can decide what to do? | Pick it up and check if there's money inside before deciding what to do? | Pick it up and shout out loud, "Has anyone lost a wallet?" | Hand it in at the nearest shop? |

# Appendix A
## Session Icons

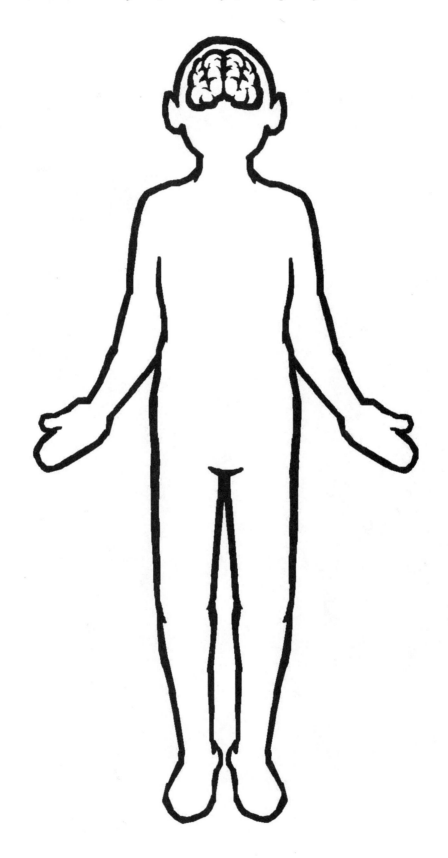

# Appendix B
# Suggested Role-Play Situations

In role-playing, it is important to choose situations that relate to participants' own lives. A number of the situations presented as suggested exercises can also serve as situations to be analyzed because they often contain more perception elements (social signals) than the topic of the day. It is possible to read the situations aloud, but it is better to role-play them. Merely reading them may underemphasize the emotional aspect of the situations. The suggested situations may be expanded to include more points (e.g., a cognitive distortion could be included in one of the roles). Notice that the examples in generally involve the majority of the topics.

### At the summer house

*(Hidden rules, culture, background variables/events, feelings)*

Carl is 17, and his girlfriend, Lisa, is 16. He's been invited by Lisa's father to spend a week at their summer house. On the final evening, Lisa's father goes to bed first, at 1 A.M. At 2 A.M., he gets up again and suggests that it's time for Carl and Lisa to go to bed. They agree. At 2:30, the father gets up again and tells them they must go to bed. He's obviously annoyed. Carl says he's 17 years old and can decide himself when to go to bed, then calls the father a senile old fool. Lisa's father tells Carl to do as he's told. Carl gets angry, moves toward the father, and says he doesn't give a damn what the father says.

### Exchanging shoes

*(Open and hidden rules, norms, cultural misunderstandings/differences, feelings)*

Brian is 15. He's just bought new shoes. He wears the shoes on a hike in the forest and gets a blister. He then goes back to the shop to exchange the shoes. The shop assistant says he can't. Brian calls the shop assistant an idiot, angrily repeats that he wants to exchange the shoes, and bangs on the counter. The shop assistant asks him to calm down. Brian then grabs hold of the man's sweater and says he'll be in for a rough time if he doesn't let him have new shoes.

### At an institution

*(Cultural misunderstandings, open and hidden rules, feelings)*

Norman is 17 and lives in an institution. Linda is 40 and one of the staff. She's making the dinner. Norman pats her bottom and says, "Hey babe, what are we having for dinner?"

## On the bus: Situation 1

*(Hidden rules, background variables/events, feelings)*

John is sitting on the bus, and a man sits down next to him. There are plenty of vacant seats in the bus. The man asks John how he's doing. John gives a sharp reply, then turns and stares out the window.

## On the bus: Situation 2

*(Culture, background variables, rules, feelings, intentions)*

Eric lives in a children's home. He's going to a rock concert in town and has been given a bus ticket, which one of the staff said is valid for the whole evening. When he gets on the bus, the driver brusquely refuses to let him travel.

## The rock group

*(Intentions, feelings, background variables)*

George and Paul play in the same group. Paul is always criticizing George for the way he plays the guitar.

## An agreement

*(Feelings, open and hidden rules, setting events, intentions, right time and place)*

Linda and her father, Stuart, have an agreement that Linda must be home by 11 P.M. Stuart sits and waits for her, and she turns up at 11:45. Stuart shouts at her that she never sticks to agreements.

## Waking up

*(Feelings, intentions, open and hidden rules, setting events)*

Lorna is 15 and lives with her mother. She has to go to school and her mother wakes her up at 7 A.M. Lorna doesn't get up, and her mother goes in again ten minutes later. She shakes Lorna and yells that she must get up. Lorna shouts back at her mother to get out of her room.

## Cinema

*(Open and hidden rules, cultural differences, feelings, thoughts–feeling–body language–action, setting events)*

Peter is 13 and is going to the movies with two friends. On his way into the cinema, the doorman stops him and asks for his ID. Peter says he doesn't have one. The man asks how old he is. Peter says he's 15. The doorman says he doesn't believe he's as old as that so he can't enter the cinema. Peter complains that it's not fair, because his friends of the same age got in. The doorman tells Peter to leave. Peter gesticulates, goes up to the doorman, and calls him an idiot.

### Tidying up

*(Hidden rules, setting events, thoughts–feelings–body language–action)*

Peter's mother tells him to tidy up his things. Peter says he'll do it later. His mother raises her voice and says he must do it now. Peter looks at his mother, and carries on watching TV. His mother goes and turns off the TV. Peter tells her sharply to put it back on. His mother repeats that he's to tidy up now. Peter gets up, points at his mother, and says: "Turn on the TV now!"

### Waiting

*(Hidden rules, intentions, feelings, background variables/events)*

Carol and Steve are 15 and dating. Steve turns up 20 minutes late for a date. Carol says he doesn't love her if he can't be bothered to get to a date on time. Steve says she's overreacting, always wanting to argue about trivial things, and needs to get real. Carol raises her voice and says he's the one who needs to get real. Steve says he can't be bothered with another argument.

### Work

*(Setting events, thoughts-feelings–body language–action, intentions)*

Sam is 18 and has an alcohol problem. He is pleased to have gotten a job in supported employment. His boss has said that he must stay sober and that if they suspect he's been drinking, he'll have to take a blood test. Last night Sam had a few beers with some friends, but as he was afraid of losing his job, he stopped drinking at midnight and went home. This morning he didn't feel too great, but decided to go to work. When he arrived, his boss asked if he was sober. Sam got a bit annoyed and said yes. The boss said he wasn't sure, so Sam would have to take a blood test.

### Ex-girlfriend

*(Hidden rules, feelings, intentions, background variables/events)*

Kate is visiting her boyfriend, Larry. She's in his bedroom when his telephone rings. As he's out just then, she answers it. It's Larry's ex-girlfriend. When Larry comes back, Kate asks why his ex-girlfriend is calling him. Larry raises his voice and says it's not her business to take his calls. Kate answers brusquely that he's changing the subject and that she wants to know if there's anything between him and his ex.

# Appendix C
## Social Perception Training Implementation Forms

# Social Perception Training Log

Name _____ Session no. _____ Date _____

1.  What happened?



2.  Did you identify any emotions in the other person?



3.  What emotions did you have yourself?



4.  What open or hidden rules could be present in the situation?



5.  Did you identify any cultural aspects that influenced the situation?



6.  What possible setting events could have influenced the other's reaction?



7.  What possible setting events could have influenced your actions?



8.  Did you experience that your thoughts influenced your emotions, body feelings, or your actions?



9.  What intentions do you think the other person had in the situation?

10. What intentions did you have in the situation?

11. Did you identify any thoughts or statements that could be considered cognitive distortions during the situation?

12. Did you identify any example of bad timing in the situation?

13. Did you ask or do anything to clarify the situation to understand it better?

14. What consequences did the interaction lead to?

15. What can I say/say to myself when I succeed?

16. What can I do better next time?

17. What can the other person do better next time?

18. How did I handle the situation? (Circle one.)

          1    2    3    4    5    6    7    8    9   10
          Badly                                  Very well

# Social Perception Training Reflection Form

| Actor 1 | Actor 2 |
|---|---|
| What happened? | What happened? |
| Emotions: | Emotions: |
| Open and hidden rules: | Open and hidden rules: |
| Cultural differences: | Cultural differences: |
| Setting events: | Setting events: |
| Expectations: | Expectations: |
| Intentions: | Intentions: |
| Cognitive distortions: | Cognitive distortions: |
| Timing: | Timing: |
| Consequences: | Consequences: |
| Solution for new start or continued role-play for Actor 1? | Solution for new start or continued role-play for Actor 1? |

From *Social Perception Training,* by K. K. Gundersen, B. Strømgren, & I. moynahan, © 2013, Champaign, IL: Research Press (800-519-2707, www.researchpress.com).

# Appendix D
## Social Perception Training Fidelity Forms

# Social Perception Training Facilitator's Evaluation Form

Facilitators _____

Date _____ Session no. _____

|  |  | Yes | No | Partly |
|---|---|:---:|:---:|:---:|
| **Introduction** | | | | |
| i | If there were issues from the last session, was a follow-up done? | ❏ | ❏ | ❏ |
| ii | Were the group rules reviewed? | ❏ | ❏ | ❏ |
| iii | Were the previous session(s) reviewed? | ❏ | ❏ | ❏ |
| iv | Was the Social Perception Training Log (provided in Appendix C) reviewed? | ❏ | ❏ | ❏ |
| v | Did the facilitators introduce an optical illusion or game? | ❏ | ❏ | ❏ |
| **Step 1: Facilitators present the topic of the day** | | | | |
| 1.1 | Did the facilitators present the topic in a logical way? | ❏ | ❏ | ❏ |
| 1.2 | Did the facilitators emphasize relevant parts of the topic? | ❏ | ❏ | ❏ |
| 1.3 | Were relevant examples used? | ❏ | ❏ | ❏ |
| 1.4 | Were visual aids like pictures or video clips used? | ❏ | ❏ | ❏ |
| 1.5 | Was the topic illustrated by games or small role-plays? | ❏ | ❏ | ❏ |
| 1.6 | Did the facilitators help to identify the need for the topic (why the topic is important)? | ❏ | ❏ | ❏ |
| 1.7 | Did the facilitators help to define possible situations in which the session topic is important? | ❏ | ❏ | ❏ |
| **Step 2: Facilitators present one situation** | | | | |
| 2.1 | Did the facilitators use a relevant example? | ❏ | ❏ | ❏ |
| 2.2. | Was the situation clearly demonstrated? | ❏ | ❏ | ❏ |
| **Step 3: Participants analyze the situation** | | | | |
| 3.1 | Was the situation analyzed from the perspective of all involved? | ❏ | ❏ | ❏ |
| 3.2 | Was the situation analyzed with respect to the content of previous sessions? | ❏ | ❏ | ❏ |
| 3.3 | Was the analysis clearly structured on PowerPoint or in another whole-group display? | ❏ | ❏ | ❏ |
| **Step 4: Participants suggest alternative ways of continuing the role-play** | | | | |
| 4.1 | Were the different suggestions written on PowerPoint or another whole-group display? | ❏ | ❏ | ❏ |
| 4.2 | Did the suggestions involve both continuing role-play and an alternative start to the role-play? | ❏ | ❏ | ❏ |
| 4.3 | Did the alternative role-play suggestions involve both (all) role-players? | ❏ | ❏ | ❏ |

|  | Yes | No | Partly |
|---|---|---|---|

### Step 5: Participants choose one solution

5.1 Did the facilitators help the participant to discuss and determine a solution? ❏ ❏ ❏

5.2 Did the facilitators emphasize the topic of the day as important to come up with a good solution? ❏ ❏ ❏

5.3 Did the facilitators contribute to a solution that was best for all? ❏ ❏ ❏

5.4 Was the new solution for all involved clearly written on PowerPoint or another whole-group display? ❏ ❏ ❏

### Step 6: Participants plan and role-play the chosen solution

6.1 Did the facilitators clearly instruct the participants in how the chosen solution should be role-played (including the use of microskills)? ❏ ❏ ❏

6.2 Did the facilitators ask participants to observe for completion of relevant topic- and microskill-specific tasks? ❏ ❏ ❏

6.3 Did the facilitators discuss the importance of the observer tasks that were assigned? ❏ ❏ ❏

### Step 7: Facilitators and participants conduct feedback round

7.1 Did the facilitators conduct the feedback round in the right sequence (observers, facilitators, actors)? ❏ ❏ ❏

7.2 Did the facilitators ensure that the observers make their comments directly to the role-players? ❏ ❏ ❏

7.3 Did all participants provide performance feedback? ❏ ❏ ❏

7.4 Did the facilitators use terms describing character (you showed respect, you were brave) when giving comments to the role-players? ❏ ❏ ❏

### Step 8: Facilitators and participants repeat Steps 4–7

8.1 If time allowed, did the facilitators include all steps (4–7) in a new role-play? ❏ ❏ ❏

### Step 9: Facilitators assign homework

9.1 Was the Social Perception Training Log (provided in Appendix C) distributed to the participants? ❏ ❏ ❏

### Review and closing

i Did the facilitators review the most important things that were learned in the session? ❏ ❏ ❏

ii Did the facilitators give an orientation to the following session? ❏ ❏ ❏

iii Did the facilitators conduct a friendship round, provide summary with evaluation, or provide other closure activities for the participants? ❏ ❏ ❏

# Social Perception Training Observer's Checklist

Facilitators _____ Date _____

Observer _____ Session no. _____

Using the following criteria, please assess how effectively the facilitator and co-facilitator conducted the Social Perception Training group.

| | Highly competent | Competent | Mildly competent | Not competent |
|---|---|---|---|---|
| 1. Demonstrated knowledge of the content presented. | 1 | 2 | 3 | 4 |
| 2. Kept up an appropriate pace during the presentation. | 1 | 2 | 3 | 4 |
| 3. Used platform skills (body, hands, eye contact, facial expression, voice). | 1 | 2 | 3 | 4 |
| 4. Related to participants and kept them interested and involved. | 1 | 2 | 3 | 4 |
| 5. Explained theory with practical examples. | 1 | 2 | 3 | 4 |
| 6. Used visuals to support the presentation and clarify concepts. | 1 | 2 | 3 | 4 |
| 7. Conveyed enthusiasm and a belief in what was presented. | 1 | 2 | 3 | 4 |
| 8. Organized and structured the session (followed established procedure). | 1 | 2 | 3 | 4 |

Observer's feedback and recommendations:

Observer's comments and recommendations received:

_____    _____

(Facilitator signature and date)    (Co-facilitator signature and date)

From *Social Perception Training,* by K. K. Gundersen, B. Strømgren, & I. moynahan, © 2013, Champaign, IL: Research Press (800-519-2707, www.researchpress.com).

# References

Akhtar, N., & Bradley, E. J. (1991). Social information processing deficits of aggressive children: Present findings and implication for social skills training. *Clinical Psychology Review, 11,* 621–644.

Albert, R. D. (1983). The Intercultural Sensitizer or Culture Assimilator: A cognitive approach. In D. Landis & R. W. Brislin (Eds.), *Handbook of intercultural training* (Vol. 2). New York: Pergamon.

Amidon, E., Roth, J., & Greenberg, M. (1991). *Group magic.* St. Paul, MN: Paul S. Amidon & Associates.

Anderson, C. A., & Bushman, B. J. (2002). Human aggression. *Annual Review of Psychology, 53,* 27–51.

Anderson, C. A., & Dill, K. E. (2000). Video games and aggressive thoughts, feelings and behavior in the laboratory and in life. *Journal of Personality and Social Psychology, 78,* 772–790.

Argyle, M. (1983). *The psychology of interpersonal behaviour* (4th ed.). Harmondsworth, Middlesex, England: Penguin Books.

Argyle, M., & Kendon, A. (1967). The experimental analysis of social performance. In L. Berkowitz (Ed.), *Advances in experimental social psychology* (Vol. 3, pp. 55–97). New York: Academic Press.

Arsenio, W. F., & Lemerise, E. A. (2004). Aggression and moral development: Integrating social information processing and moral domain models. *Child Development, 75,* 987–1002.

Bandura, A. (1977a). Self-efficacy: Toward a unifying theory of behavioral change. *Psychological Review, 84,* 191–215.

Bandura, A. (1977b). *Social learning theory.* Englewood Cliffs, NJ: Prentice Hall.

Bandura, A. (1986). *Social foundations of thought and action: A social-cognitive theory.* Englewood Cliffs, NJ: Prentice Hall.

Bandura, A. (2006). Autobiography. In M. G. Lindzey & W. M. Runyan (Eds.), *A history of psychology in autobiography* (Vol. 9). Washington, DC: American Psychological Association.

Barriga, A. Q., Morrison, E. M., Liau, A. K., & Gibbs, J. C. (2000). Moral cognition: Explaining the gender difference in antisocial behavior. *Merrill-Palmer Quarterly, 47,* 532–562.

Bellack, A. S., Mueser, K., Gingerich, S., & Agresta, J. (1997). *Social skills training for schizophrenia: A step-by-step guide.* New York: Guilford.

Bellack, A. S., Mueser, K. T., Gingerich, S., & Agresta, J. (2004). *Social skills training for schizophrenia: A step-by-step guide* (2nd ed.). New York: Guilford.

Bijou, S. W., & Baer D. M. (1961). *Child development: I. A systematic and empirical theory.* Englewood Cliffs, NJ: Prentice Hall.

Binder, C. (1996). Behavioral fluency: Evolution of a new paradigm. *The Behavior Analyst, 19,* 163–197.

Brown, H., & Ciuffetelli, D. C. (Eds.). (2009). *Foundational methods: Understanding teaching and learning.* Toronto: Pearson Education.

Brown, P., & Fraser, C. (1979). Speech as a marker of situations. In K. Scherer & H. Giles (Eds.), *Social markers in speech.* Cambridge: Cambridge University Press.

Buck, R. (1984). What are the similarities and differences in facial behavior across cultures? New York: Guilford.

Burns, D. D. (1980). *Feeling good: The new mood therapy.* New York: New American Library.

Calame, R., & Parker, K. (2013). *Family TIES: A family-based intervention to complement Prepare©, ART©, and TIES youth groups.* Champaign, IL: Research Press.

Carlson, M., Marcus-Newhall, A., & Miller, N. (1990). Effects of situational aggression cues: A quantitative review. *Journal of Personality and Social Psychology, 58,* 622–633.

Carr, E. G., Reeve, C. E., & Magito-McLaughlin, D. (1996). Contextual influences on problem behaviour in people with developmental disabilities. In L. K. Koegel, R. L. Koegel, & G. Dunlap (Eds.), *Positive behavioural support: Including people with difficult behaviour in the community.* Baltimore: Paul H. Brookes.

Chandler, L. K., Fowler, S. A., & Lubeck, R. C. (1992). An analysis of the effects of mulitiple setting events on the social behavior of preschool children with special needs. *Journal of Behavior Analysis, 25,* 281–288.

Chang, E. C., D'Zurilla, T. J., & Sanna, L. J. (2004). *Social problem solving: Theory, research and training.* Washington DC: American Psychological Association.

Crick, N. R., & Dodge, K. A. (1994). A review and reformulation of social information-processing mechanisms in children's social adjustment. *Psychological Bulletin, 115,* 74–101.

Crick, N. R., & Dodge, K. A. (1996). Social information-processing mechanisms on reactive and proactive aggression. *Child Development 67,* 993–1002.

Darley, J. M., & Fazio, R. H. (1980). Expectancy confirmation processes arising in the social interaction sequence. *American Psychologist, 35,* 867–881.

Davey, L., Day, A., & Howells, K. (2005). Anger, over-control and serious violent offending. *Aggressive and Violent Behaviour, 10,* 624–635.

Denham, S. A., Blair, K. A., DeMulder, E., Levitas, J., Sawyer, K. et al. (2003). Preschool emotional competence: Pathway to social competence? *Child Development, 74,* 238–256.

DeRosier, M. E. (2004). Building relationships and combating bullying: Effectiveness of a school-based social skills group intervention. *Journal of Clinical Child and Adolescent Psychology, 33,* 196–201.

DiBiase, A. M., Gibbs, J. C., Potter, G. B., & Blount, M. R. (2012). *Teaching adolescents to think and act responsibly: The EQUIP approach.* Champaign, IL: Research Press.

DiDonato, N. C. (2013). Effective self- and co-regulation in collaborative learning groups: An analysis of how students regulate problem solving of authentic interdisciplinary tasks. *Instructional Science: An International Journal of the Learning Sciences, 41*(1), 25–47.

Dodge, K. A. (2006). Translational science in action: Hostile attributional style and the development of aggressive behavior problems. *Development and Psychopathology, 18,* 791–814.

Dodge, K. A., Price, J. M., Bachorowski, J., & Newman, J. P. (1990). Hostile attributional tendencies in highly aggressive adolecents. *Journal of Abnormal Psychology, 99,* 385–392.

Ekman, P., Friesen, W. V., & Ellsworth, P. (1982). What are the similarities and differences in facial behavior across cultures? In P. Ekman (Ed.), *Emotion in the human face* (pp. 128–143). Cambridge: Cambridge University Press.

Elliott, S. N., & Gresham, F. M. (1991). *Social skills intervention guide: Practical strategies for social skills training.* Circle Pines, MN: American Guidance Service.

Fabes, R. A., Eisenberg, N., Jones, S., Smith, M., Guthrie, I., Poulin, R. et al. (1999). Regulation, emotionality, and preschoolers' socially competent peer interactions. *Child Development, 70,* 432–442.

Fixsen, D. L., Naoom, S. F., Blase, K. A., Friedman, R. M., & Wallace, F. (2005). *Implementation research: A synthesis of the literature.* Tampa: University of South Florida, Louis de la Parte Florida Mental Health Institute, The National Implementation Research Network (FMHI Publication #231).

Foster, S. L., & Crain, M. M. (2002). Social skills and problem-solving training. In F. W. Kaslow & T. Patterson (Eds.), *Comprehensive handbook of psychotherapy: Cognitive-behavioral approaches.* New York: Wiley.

Fox, J., & Conroy, M. (1995). Setting events and behavioral disorders of children and youth: An interbehavioral field analysis for research and practice. *Journal of Emotional and Behavioral Disorders, 3,* 130–140.

Frydenberg, E. (1997). *Adolescent coping: Theoretical and research perspectives.* London: Routledge.

Gaffney, L. R., Thorpe, K., Young, R., Collett, R., & Occhipinti, S. (1998). Social skills, expectancies, and drinking in adolescents. *Addictive Behavior, 23,* 587–599.

Gibbs, J. C. (1993). Moral-cognitive interventions. In A. P. Goldstein & C. R. Huff (Eds.), *The gang intervention handbook* (pp. 159–185). Champaign, IL: Research Press.

Gibbs, J. C. (1996). Sociomoral group treatment for young offenders. In C. R. Hollin & K. Howells (Eds.), *Clinical approaches to working with young offenders* (pp. 129–149). Chichester, England: Wiley.

Gibbs, J. C., Potter, G. B., & Goldstein, A. P. (1995). *The EQUIP program: Teaching youth to think and act responsibly through a peer-helping approach.* Champaign IL: Research Press.

Glick, B., & Gibbs, J. C. (2011). *Aggression Replacement Training: A comprehensive intervention for aggressive youth* (3rd ed.). Champaign, IL: Research Press.

Goldstein, A. P. (1988). *The Prepare Curriculum: Teaching prosocial competencies.* Champaign, IL: Research Press.

Goldstein, A. P. (1994). *The ecology of aggression.* New York: Plenum.

Goldstein, A. P. (1999). *The Prepare Curriculum: Teaching prosocial competencies.* (Rev. ed.). Champaign, IL: Research Press.

Goldstein, A. P. (2004). ART and beyond: The Prepare Curriculum. In A. P. Goldstein, R. Nensen, B. Daleflod, & M. Kalt (Eds.), *New perspectives on Aggression Replacement Training.* Chichester, England: Wiley.

Goldstein, A. P., & Glick, B. (1987). *Aggression Replacement Training: A comprehensive intervention for adolescent youth.* Champaign, IL: Research Press.

Goldstein, A. P., Glick, B., Carthan, W., & Blancero, D. (1994). *The prosocial gang: Implementing Aggression Replacement Training.* Thousand Oaks, CA: Sage.

Goldstein, A. P., Glick, B., & Gibbs, J. C. (1998). *Aggression Replacement Training: A comprehensive intervention for aggressive youth.* (Rev. ed.) Champaign, IL: Research Press.

Goldstein, A. P., & McGinnis, E. (1997). *Skillstreaming the adolescent: New strategies and perspectives for teaching prosocial skills.* Champaign, IL: Research Press.

Goldstein, A. P., Nensen, R., Daleflod, B., & Kalt, M. (Eds.). (2004). *New perspectives on Aggression Replacement Training.* Chichester, England: Wiley.

Goleman, D. (2005). *Emotional intelligence: Why it can matter more than IQ.* New York: Random House.

Gresham, F. M., & Elliott, S. N. (1990). *Social Skills Rating System.* Circle Pines, MN: American Guidance Service.

Gundersen, K. (2010). Reducing behaviour problems in young people through social competence programmes. *The International Journal of Emotional Education, 2,* 48–62.

Gundersen, K., & moynahan, l. (2003). Trening av sosial kompetanse [Training in social competence]. In F. Svartdal & S. Eikeseth (Eds.), *Anvendt atferdsanlayse: Teori og praksis* [Applied behavior analysis: Theory and practice] (pp. 293–316). Oslo, Norway: Gyldendal Akademisk.

Gundersen, K., & Valgjord, L. (2011). *Sosial persepsjonstrening: Trenermanual* [Social perception training: Manual for facilitators]. Oslo, Norway: Diakonhjemmet University College.

Hall, C. W. (2006). Self-reported aggression and the perception of anger in facial expression photos: Erratum. *Journal of Psychology: Interdisciplinary and Applied, 140,* 395–396.

Hall, E. T. (1966). *The hidden dimension.* New York: Doubleday.

Hallberstadt, A. G., Denham, S. A., & Dunsmore, J. C. (2001). Affective social competence. *Social Development, 10,* 79–119.

Hatcher, R. M., & Hollin, C. R. (2005). The identification and management of anti-social and offending behaviour. In J. Winstone & F. Pakes (Eds.), *Community justice: Issues for probation and community justice* (pp. 165–182). Cullompton, England: Willan Press.

Hay, D. F., Payne, A., & Chadwick, A. (2004). Peer relations in childhood. *Journal of Child Psychology and Psychiatry, 45,* 84–108.

Heider, F. (1958). The psychology of interpersonal relations. New York: Wiley.

Hollin, C. R. (1990). *Cognitive behavioral interventions with young offenders.* Elmsford, NY: Pergamon Press.

Hollin, C. R. (1999). Treatment programs for offenders. Meta-analysis, "what works," and beyond. *International Journal of Law and Psychiatry, 22,* 361–372.

Hollin, C. R. (2004). The cognitive-behavioral context. In A. P. Goldstein, R. Nensen, B. Daleflod, & M. Kalt (Eds.), *New perspectives on Aggression Replacement Training* (pp. 3–19). Chichester, England: John Wiley & Sons.

Hollin, C. R., & Bloxsom, C. A. J. (2007). Treatments for angry aggression. In T. A. Gannon, T. Ward, A. R. Beech, & D. Fisher (Eds.), *Aggressive offenders' cognition: Theory, research and practice* (pp. 215–229). Chichester, England: Wiley.

Hollin, C. R., & Palmer, E. J. (2001). Skills training. In C. R. Hollin (Ed.), *Handbook of offender assessment and treatment.* Chichester, England: John Wiley & Sons.

Hollin, C. R., & Palmer, E. J. (2006a). The Adolescent Problems Inventory: A profile of incarcerated English young male offenders. *Personality and Individual Differences, 40,* 1485–1495.

Hollin, C. R., & Palmer, E. J. (Eds). (2006b). *Offending behaviour programmes: Development, application, and controversies.* Chichester, England: Wiley.

Hollin, C. R., & Trower, P. (Eds.). (1986a). *Handbook of social skills training: Vol. 1. Applications across the life span.* Oxford, England: Pergamon Press.

Hollin, C. R., & Trower, P. (Eds.). (1986b). *Handbook of social skills training: Vol. 2. Clinical applications and new directions.* Oxford, England: Pergamon Press.

Johnson, D. W., Johnson, R. T., & Stanne, M. B. (2000). *Cooperative learning methods: A meta-analysis.* Cooperative Learning Center, University of Minnesota.

Jolliffe, D., & Farrington, D. P. (2007). Examining the relationship between low empathy and self-reported offending. *Legal and Criminological Psychology, 12,* 265–286.

Jones, W. H., Hobbs, S. A., & Hockenbury, D. (1982). Loneliness and social skill deficits. *Journal of Personality and Social Psychology, 42,* 682–689.

Kohlberg, L. (1978). Revisions in the theory and practice of mental development. In W. Damon (Ed.), *New directions in child development: Moral development* (Vol. 2, pp. 83–88). San Francisco: Jossey-Bass.

Lemerise, E. A., & Arsenio, W. F. (2000). An integrated model of emotion processes and cognition in social information processing. *Child Development, 71,* 107–118.

Lipsey, M. W., & Wilson, D. B. (1998). Effective intervention for serious juvenile offenders. In R. Loeber & D. Farrington (Eds.), *Serious and violent juvenile offenders: Risk factors and successful interventions* (pp. 313–345). Thousand Oaks, CA: Sage.

Lipton, D. M., McDonel, E. C., & McFall, R. M. (1987). Heterosocial perception in rapists. *Journal of Consulting and Clinical Psychology, 55,* 17–21.

Lösel, F., & Beelmann, A. (2005). Social-problem-solving programs for preventing antisocial behavior in children and youth. In M. McMurran & J. McGuire (Eds.), *Social problem solving and offending: Evidence, evaluation, and evolution* (pp. 127–143). Chichester, England: Wiley.

Lösel, F., Bliesener, T., & Bender, D. (2007). Social information processing, experiences of aggression in social contexts, and aggressive behavior in adolescents. *Criminal Justice and Behavior, 34,* 330-347.

Marcus-Newhall, A., Pedersen, W. C., Carlson, M., & Miller, N. (2000). Displaced aggression is alive and well: A meta-analytic review. *Journal of Personality and Social Psychology, 78,* 670–689.

McCown, W., Johnson, J., & Austin, S. (1986). Inability of delinquents to recognize facial affects. *Journal of Social Behavior and Personality 1,* 489–496.

McGinnis, E. (2012a). *Skillstreaming the adolescent: A guide for teaching prosocial skills* (3rd ed.). Champaign, IL: Research Press.

McGinnis, E. (2012b). *Skillstreaming the elementary school child: A guide for teaching prosocial skills* (3rd ed.). Champaign, IL: Research Press.

McGinnis, E., & Goldstein, A. P. (1997). *Skillstreaming the elementary school child: New strategies and perspectives for teaching prosocial skills* (2nd ed.). Champaign, IL: Research Press.

McGuire, J. (2005). Social problem solving: Basic concepts, research, and applications. In M. McMurran (Ed.), *Social problem solving and offending: Evidence, evaluation, and evolution* (pp. 3–29). Chichester, England: Wiley.

Miller, P. A., & Eisenberg, N. (1988). The relation of empathy to aggressive and externalizing/antisocial behaviour. *Psychological Bulletin, 103,* 324–344.

Morrison, R. L., & Bellack, A. S. (1981). The role of social perception in social skills. *Behavior Therapy, 12,* 69–79.

moynahan, l. (2003). Enhanced Aggression Replacement Training with children and youth with autism spectrum disorder. *Reclaiming Children and Youth 12*(3), 174–180.

Nelson, J. R., Smith, D. J., & Dodd, J. (1990). The moral reasoning of juvenile delinquents: A meta-analysis. *Journal of Abnormal Child Psychology, 18,* 709–727.

Nietzel, M. T., Hasemann, D. M., & Lynam, D. R. (1999). Behavioral perspective on violent behavior. In V. B. Van Hasselt & M. Hersen (Eds.), *Handbook of psychological approaches with violent offenders: Contemporary strategies and issues* (pp. 39–66). New York: Kluwer Academic/Plenum.

Nisbett, R. E., & Cohen, D. (1996). *Culture of honor: The psychology of violence in the South.* Boulder, CO: Westview.

Njardvik, U., Matson, J. L., & Cherry, K. E. (1999). A comparison of social skills in adults with autistic disorder, pervasive developmental disorder not otherwise specified, and mental retardation. *Journal of Autism and Developmental Disorders, 29,* 287–295.

Novaco, R. W. (1975). *Anger control: The development and evaluation of an experimental treatment.* Lexington, MA: D. C. Heath.

Novaco, R. W. (2007). Anger dysregulation. In T. Cavell & K. Malcolm (Eds.), *Anger, aggression, and interventions for interpersonal violence* (pp. 3–54). Mahwah, NJ: Erlbaum.

Novaco, R. W., & Welsh, W. N. (1989). Anger disturbances: Cognitive mediation and clinical prescriptions. In K. Howells & C. R. Hollin (Eds.), *Clinical approaches to violence.* Chichester, England: Wiley.

Nowicki, S., & Duke, M. P. (1992). *Helping the child who doesn't fit in.* Atlanta: Peachtree.

O'Donohue, W., & Krasner, L. (1995). Psychological skills training. In W. O'Donohue & L. Krasner (Eds.), *Handbook of psychological skills training.* Boston: Allyn and Bacon.

Olsen, T. M., & Gundersen, K. K. (2012). *Implementering av ART* [Implementation of ART]. Oslo, Norway: Diakonhjemmet University College.

O'Reilly, M. F. (1995). Functional analysis and treatment of escape-maintained aggression correlated with sleep deprivation. *Journal of Applied Behavior Analysis, 28,* 225–226.

Palmer, E. J. (2003). *Offending behaviour: Moral reasoning, criminal conduct and the rehabilitation of offenders.* Cullompton, England: Willan Press.

Palmer, E. J., & Hollin, C. R. (1996). Assessing adolescent problems: An overview of the adolescent problems inventory. *Journal of Adolescence, 19,* 347–354.

Palmer, E. J., & Hollin, C. R. (1999). Social competence and sociomoral reasoning in young offenders. *Applied Cognitive Psychology, 13,* 79–87.

Patel, N. M. (2004). *The impact of social-cognitive skills on social competence in persons with mental retardation.* Dissertation Abstracts International: Section B. The Sciences and Engineering, Vol. 65 (3-B).

Payne, A. A., Gottfredson, D. C., & Gottfredson, G. D. (2006). Implementation of school-based prevention programs: Results from a national study. *Prevention Science, 7,* 225–237.

Phillips, E. L. (1985). Social skills: History and prospect. In L. L'Abate & M. A. Milan (Eds.), *Handbook of social skills training and research* (pp. 3–21). New York: Wiley.

Piaget, J. (1932). *The moral judgement of the child.* London: Routledge and Kegan Paul.

Ratey, J. (2008). *SPARK: The revolutionary new science of exercise and the brain.* New York: Little, Brown.

Rosenthal, R., & Jacobsen, L. (1968). *Pygmalion in the classroom: Teacher expectation and student intellectual development.* New York: Holt, Rinehart & Winston.

Schlundt, D. G., & McFall, R. M. (1985). New directions in the assessment of social competence and social skills. In L. L'Abate & M. A. Milan (Eds.), *Handbook of social skills training and research* (pp. 22–49). New York: Wiley.

Schmitt, B. D. (1999). *Your child's health.* New York: Bantam.

Shure, M. B. (2001). *I Can Problem Solve: An interpersonal cognitive-behavioral problem-solving program—Intermediate elementary grades.* Champaign, IL: Research Press.

Spence, S. H. (1981a). Differences in social skills performance between institutionalized juvenile male offenders and a comparable group of boys without offence records. *British Journal of Clinical Psychology, 20,* 163–171.

Spence, S. H. (1981b). Validation of social skills of adolescent males in an interview conversation with a previously unknown adult. *Journal of Applied Behavior Analysis, 14,* 159–168.

Stams, G. J., Brugman, D., Dekovic, M., van Rosmale, L., van der Laan, P., & Gibbs, J. C. (2006). The moral judgment of juvenile delinquents: A meta-analysis. *Journal of Abnormal Child Psychology, 34,* 697–713.

Stifter, C. A. (2002), Individual differences in emotion regulation in infancy: A thematic collection. *Infancy, 3,* 129–132.

Strømgren, B., Gundersen, K. K., & Svartal, F. (2013). *Evaluation of the SPT program.* Unpublished manuscript.

Svartdal, F. (2011). Bevissthet og bevissthetstilstander. [Consciousness and states of consciousness] In F. Svartdal (Ed.), *Psykologi 1: En introduksjon* [Psychology 1: An introduction] (pp. 73–87). Oslo, Norway: Gyldendal.

Swaffer, T., & Hollin, C. R. (2000). Anger and impulse control. In R. Newell & K. Gournay (Eds.), *Mental health nursing: An evidence-based approach* (pp. 265–289). Edinburgh: Churchill Livingstone.

Swaffer, T., & Hollin, C. R. (2001). Anger and general health in young offenders. *Journal of Forensic Psychiatry, 12,* 90–103.

Tate, D. C., Reppucci, N. D., & Mulvey, E. P. (1995). Violent juvenile delinquents: Treatment effectiveness and implications for future action. *American Psychologist, 50,* 777–781.

Thompson, P., & White, S. (2010). Play and positive group dynamics. *Reclaiming Children and Youth, 19*(3), 53–57.

Tse, W. S., & Bond, A. J. (2004). The impact of depression on social skills. *Journal of Nervous and Mental Disorders, 192,* 260–268.

Tuckman, B. W. (1965). Developmental sequences in small groups. *Psychological Bulletin, 63,* 384–399.

Tuckman, B. W., & Jensen, M. A. (1977). Stages of small group development revisited. *Group and Organization, 2,* 419–427.

Veneziano, C., & Veneziano, L. (1988). Knowledge of social skills among institutionalized juvenile delinquents: An assessment. *Criminal Justice and Behaviour, 15,* 152–171.

Waldman, I. D. (1996). Aggressive boys' hostile perceptual and response biases: The role of attention and impulsivity. *Child Development, 67,* 1015–1033.

Ward, C. I., & McFall, R. M. (1986). Further validation of the Problem Inventory for Adolescent Girls: Comparing Caucasian and black delinquents and nondelinquents. *Journal of Consulting and Clinical Psychology, 54,* 732–733.

Weiss, B., Dodge, K. A., Bates, J. E., & Pettit, G. S. (1992). Some consequences of early harsh discipline: Child aggression and a maladaptive social information processing style. *Child Development, 63,* 1321–1335.

Whaler, R. G., & Graves, M. G. (1983). Setting events in social networks: Ally or enemy in child behavior therapy? *Behavior Therapy, 14,* 19–36.

Wilson, S. J., & Lipsey, M. V. (2007). School-based interventions for aggressive and disruptive behavior: Update of a meta-analysis. *American Journal of Preventive Medicine, 33,* 130–143.

# About the Editors

**MARK AMENDOLA,** LCW, started his career as a child care counselor at a residential treatment center in 1980 after earning a bachelor's degree from Gannon University in Erie, Pennsylvania. He served in a variety of roles, including counseling with delinquent youth in a day treatment program and as a mental health therapist and supervisor in a partial hospitalization program. He worked for Erie County, Pennsylvania, as a supervisor, authorizing treatment and providing quality management for residential and community-based programming. He has served as Executive Director of Perseus House, Inc., and Charter School of Excellence in Erie, Pennsylvania, since 1994 and 2002, respectively. He completed his graduate degree from Case Western University in 1990 and maintains a private practice that serves youth and adults.

**ROBERT OLIVER,** EdD, started his career as a child care counselor in an intensive treatment unit for delinquent youth. He spent multiple years as a mental health specialist and then worked in the capacity of supervisor of a partial hospitalization program. He began working in the school district of the City of Erie in 1989, serving as Principal of Alternative Education, Supervisor of Student Assistance Programs, Dean of Northwest Pennsylvania Collegiate Academy, Director of High Schools, and Assistant Superintendent. He is currently the Chief Educational Officer of the Perseus House Charter School of Excellence in Erie, Pennsylvania.

# About the Authors

**KNUT KORNELIUS GUNDERSEN** is professor at the Centre for Social Competence at Diakonhjemmet University College in Sandnes, Norway. He has written several books and scientific articles in the area of social competence, environmental therapy, and social networking. He has also presented at national and international congresses in 14 different countries and is one of the key persons involved in the training and implementation of ART and Prepare Curriculum components in Norway, Iceland, Finland, Denmark, and Russia. Knut is also president of the PREPSEC International board, which has the aim of disseminating programs for training social competences, including Prepare programs. Knut has also been an active member of the ENSEC organization, which also targets the development of social and emotional competency via a European network of experts. In addition to being the main author of the Social Perception Training program he is coauthor of the Problem-Solving Training Prepare Curriculum Implementation Guide.

**BØRGE STRØMGREN**, PHD, is an associate professor in the Faculty of Health Sciences at Oslo and Akershus University College of Applied Sciences in Norway. He has conducted research on Aggression Replacement Training (ART) in Norwegian schools and currently investigates schoolwide intervention programs and implementation of ART and other social competence programs or programs aimed at improving academic functioning. His clinical practice includes consulting and hands-on supervision of interventions of programs for people with autism spectrum disorders and developmental disabilities. His main research focuses on how Positive Behavior Intervention and Support (PBIS) can effectively support the short- and long-term effects of ART. Børge is also a board member of PREPSEC International.

**LUKE MOYNAHAN** is a retired applied behavior analyst with degrees in pedagogy, psychology, and family therapy. He is a Marxist behaviorist and lives in Cuba and Tenerife. He is a former member of the advisory board of ICART and is coauthor of the book *Erstatt Aggresjon* [Replace the Aggression] and the article "Nettverk og Sosial Kompetanse" [Social Network and Social Competence]. He was also one of the contributors behind the first study plan for postgraduate education in training social competence in Norway. He has written several other articles, books, and book chapters within the area of social competence.